TWAYNE'S WORLD AUTHORS SERIES

A Survey of the World's Literature

HUNGARY

Sándor Petőfi

TWAS 587

Sándor Petőfi

SÁNDOR PETŐFI

By ENIKŐ MOLNÁR BASA

Library of Congress

TWAYNE PUBLISHERS

A DIVISION OF G. K. HALL & CO., BOSTON

Published in 1980 by Twayne Publishers,
A Division of G. K. Hall & Co.

Printed on permanent/durable acid-free paper and bound in the United States of America

First Printing

Frontispiece artwork by Miklós Barabás
reproduced from the collection of the Library of Congress

Library of Congress Cataloging in Publication Data

Basa, Enikő, M
Sandor Petofi.
(Twayne's world authors series ; TWAS 587 : Hungary)
Bibliography: p. 180-86
Includes index.
1. Petőfi, Sándor, 1823-1849—
Criticism and interpretation. I. Title.
PH3308.B3 894'.511'12 79-28055
ISBN 0-8057-6429-1

For my Parents

Contents

	About the Author	
	Preface	
	Chronology	
1.	Poet, Politician, Soldier	15
2.	Early Poems	34
3.	New Themes, New Styles	61
4.	Júlia Szendrey	79
5.	János Arany and the Objective Lyric	94
6.	"Freedom, Love–These Two I Must Have"	111
7.	The Last Year	135
8.	Petőfi Abroad	160
9.	Conclusion	169
	Notes and References	173
	Selected Bibliography	180
	Index	187

About the Author

Enikő Molnár Basa was born in Huszt, Hungary, in 1939. She attended schools in Germany and the United States, receiving a B.A. in English from Trinity College, Washington, D.C., and the M.A. and Ph.D. in comparative literature from the University of North Carolina, Chapel Hill. She taught at the University of Maryland, Dunbarton College, and American University, and is currently employed by the Library of Congress. Her interests are in Hungarian–English–German literary relations, particularly the nineteenth-century, and in Hungarian folklore and ethnic literature. She has published articles on the reception of English literature in Hungary and of Hungarian literature in the United States, and is presently working on a revision of her dissertation on the *poème d'humanité* and Madách's *Tragedy of Man.* These interests have also been represented in addresses delivered at various conferences. She is active in the Modern Language Association, the Southern Comparative Literature Association on whose journal she serves as associate editor, the American Hungarian Educators' Association of which she is president, and the Hungarian Studies Newsletter where she is journal editor. She is also editor for the Hungarian section of the Twayne World Authors Series.

Preface

The greatest lyric poet of nineteenth-century Hungarian literature, Sándor Petőfi, represents an individualistic blending of poetic tastes and styles which was to influence Hungarian literature for several decades. In his poetry the more positive elements of romanticism such as the return to the simplicity of the folksong and the use of the vocabulary of the "common man," as well as the concern with political and social issues, were united to a deep realism that rejected the dreamy world of romances and the sentimental concern with the past in favor of a program of reform.

Directly or indirectly, all of his writings served this end. For Petőfi, the goal and purpose of literary activity remained the uplifting of the people or the masses (*nép*, roughly equivalent to the common man), and he succeeded in having some of his contemporaries, and many successors, adopt these views. What is most amazing about the poet, however, is that he accomplished all this in less than five years, of which the last one was spent chiefly in political and military activity, and while he was under almost constant attack for the innovations he brought to the aloof, polite "almanac lyrics" fashionable at the time, as well as for his radical political and social views.

Therefore, in this work I have tried to show the poet and the man. The literary traditions of the nineteenth century formed his style, but he also helped to shape them, particularly in moving from romanticism to realism. By bringing poetry closer to everyday experience and by truly using everyday language, he put into practice Wordsworth's injunction, "to choose incidents and situations from common life and to relate or describe them throughout, as far as . . . possible, in . . . language really used by men, and, at the same time, to throw over them a certain coloring of imagination."[1] In both the use of everyday language and the heightening of the reader's awareness of ordinary objects, Petőfi prepared the way for the great lyricists of the twentieth century, Endre Ady, Attila József, and others.

Since the life of Petőfi is inseparable from his work, I have organized the chapters around the major events of his life. It was these that provided the themes, and often the inspiration, for his poetry. Similarly, the three stages of his poetic development could be delineated by reference to his life. His use of the folksong, imitative at first, reached a peak with his first successes. The second period, one of experimentation, culminated with his courtship and marriage: the poems of this period show an original use of the styles, themes and methods of the romantic lyric. Finally, in the third period, he tested the limits of the poetic conventions of his day in the great freedom of his verses as well as the wide range of his topics. Appropriately, this coincided with his involvement in the Revolution of 1848 and served as an expression of it.

Because the form and the thought are closely dependent on each other in Petőfi's poetry, I have extensively cited the works discussed. In each instance I give the original, followed by a close literal translation. I have made no attempt to reproduce the metrical qualities or the rhyme, preferring to concentrate on conveying the words, images, and ideas instead. I believe that this roughly interlinear effort best captures both the meaning and the imaginative effect. Whenever an awareness of the metrical qualities of the poem is important, I have explained these as fully as possible. Similarly, when the connotations of a Hungarian word could not be fully conveyed by the English, I have given the more literal version or discussed the emotional associations more fully.

The names of persons and places are given in Hungarian. Though in earlier criticism there was a tendency to translate the names of literary and historical figures, this is no longer accepted practice since it led to confusion. Similarly, the names of cities are in the original Hungarian, although I have given the current equivalents for some of the major ones now outside Hungary. The Hungarian names of these cities are always used in the citations.

I wish to thank the Szépirodalmi Kiadó of Budapest for permission to use their 1972 edition, *Petőfi Sándor összes költe-*

ményei, as the basis for the Hungarian quotations from Petőfi's poetry. The photograph of the frontispiece is a copy of a painting by Miklós Barabás.

Finally, my grateful thanks to all who helped me in this work: Sylvia Bowman and Alberta Hines whose patience allowed for unexpected delays and whose preliminary reading led to a more cohesive work, Paul Debreczeny for his careful reading of the manuscript and useful suggestions, Carol Éltető for typing and retyping the manuscript as it was composed, to my parents and family for their support, encouragement, and understanding.

ENIKŐ MOLNÁR BASA

Silver Spring

Chronology

1823 Sándor Petőfi is born in Kiskőrös on January 1.

1828–1838 Schooling in Kiskunfélegyháza, Kecskemét, and Sárszentlőrinc; gymnasium or high school studies at Pest, Aszód, and Selmec.

1839 Enlists as a soldier.

1841 February, medical discharge. Works as an actor. Student at the Academy in Pápa. May 22, first poem is published in the *Athenaeum*.

1842 Due to financial difficulties, is unable to resume his studies in the fall. Seeks to support himself as an actor.

1843 Works as a copyist for the *Országgyűlési Tudósítok* (*Reports on the Diet*) in Poszony (Bratislava) and translates two English novels.

1844 July 1, becomes assistant editor of the *Pesti Divatlap* (*Fashion Magazine of Pest*). Publishes *A helység-kalapácsa* (*The Hammer of the Village*) and *Versek 1842–1844* (*Poems*).

1845 *János Vitéz* and *Cipruslombok Etelke sírjáról* (*Cypress Leaves from the Tomb of Etelke*). Leaves his position with the *Pesti Divatlap* to make a tour of Northern Hungary. Publishes notes of the journey under the title "Uti jegyzetek" ("Journal notes") in the periodical, *Életkepek* (*Panorama*); October, *Szerelem gyöngyei* (*Pearls of Love*); November, *Versek II* (*Poems, II*).

1846 Forms the "Tizek Társasága" ("Society of Ten") to work for better contracts between publishers and authors. *Felhők* (*Clouds*) and the novel, *A hóhér kötele* (*The Hangman's Rope*). September, meets Júlia Szendrey. Returns to Pest to work for the *Életképek.*

1847 *Tigris és hiéna* (*The Tiger and the Hyena*) and *Összes költeményei* (*Collected Poems*). Tour of Northern Hungary. September 8, marries Júlia.

1848 Second edition of *Összes költeményei.* March 14, writes the "Nemzeti Dal" ("National Ode"); March 15, takes an active role in the Revolution. April 30, becomes associate editor of the *Életképek* with Mór Jókai. *Lapok Petőfi naplójából* (*Pages from the Diary of Petőfi*) and his translation of Shakespeare's *Coriolanus.* June 14, defeated in the elections at Szabadszállás. October 15, commissioned as a captain in the army and assigned to Debrecen. December 15, son is born.

1849 January, requests a transfer to the army of General Bem and takes part in the Transylvanian campaign. Promoted to the rank of major by Bem, he resigns his commission in the summer due to differences with the headquarters staff. July 17, rejoins the army and Bem restores his rank. July 31, participates in the Battle of Segesvár and is killed by Cossacks.

1868 Death of Júlia.

1870 Death of Petőfi's son, Zoltán.

1874 Deluxe edition of Petőfi's collected poems.

1892 First critical edition of the poet's work is begun by Adolph Havas.

CHAPTER 1

Poet, Politician, Soldier

I *From Student to Actor*

SÁNDOR Petőfi was born on January 1, 1823, in Kiskörös, a town of the Hungarian plain, to István Petrovics, innkeeper and butcher, and his wife Mária Hruz. His father's family, in spite of the Serbian name (which Petőfi was to change when he chose poetry as his vocation) had lived in Hungary for generations and even possessed a patent of nobility—now unused—granted during the Turkish wars.[1] Only once did the intensely republican poet refer to this status, and he never claimed or used its privileges. His mother, Slovak by birth, came from the Hungarian Highlands in the north. Such an ethnic mix was not unusual, and the young man grew up in what he himself considered the "most magyar" area of all Hungary, the region called Kis Kunság (Little Cumania) on the Great Plains. Much of his poetry celebrates the people and the landscape of this region. Though not the first to do so, he was more successful than earlier poets in capturing the moods of the region known as the "Alföld."

István Petrovics, well-to-do and ambitious for his sons, especially the elder one, intended to educate him for a profession.[2] He sent young Sándor to Kecskemét in 1828, and three years later to the lower gymnasium or junior high school at Sárszentlőrinc. One reason for his being sent away from home at an early age was his father's desire to send Sándor to Lutheran schools, though of the two years spent in Pest (1833–1835), the second was in the Piarist school. The choice of schools in Pest[3] was motivated by István Petrovics's conviction that a good command of German, the language of the Austrian bureaucracy and of most commerce, was necessary. Sándor thus received a good liberal education in both Hungarian and German.

In September, 1835, Petőfi transferred to Aszód, where he completed the lower classes of the gymnasium and graduated as valedictorian. This period seems to have been the happiest of his school years. He was active in various literary clubs and, through the zeal of some nationalistic teachers, became acquainted with the prominent authors of the eighteenth century: Dániel Berzsenyi, József Gvadányi, and Mihály Csokonai Vitéz as well as the popular poets of the day, Mihály Vörösmarty and József Bajza.

The year spent at Selmec, in the upper division of the gymnasium, was marred by his father's financial troubles and by Sándor's personal clashes with one of the teachers. The young man was a scholarship student and had to maintain his grades to receive aid. The conflict between him and the teacher casts some light on the political situation that was to be exploited by the Habsburgs in 1848. Daniel Lichard, a Slovak nationalist, opposed the activity of Petrovics in the Nemes Magyar Társaság (Hungarian Noble Society). As a result of these pressures, Sándor gave in to his leaning toward the theater and on February 15, 1839, when he was barely sixteen, ran away with a group of touring players.

His decision to become an actor was not taken lightly; though he had toyed with the idea earlier, he also saw the value of an education, and in fact made every effort to complete his studies when the opportunity arose later. The years that followed were particularly hard ones. Petőfi roamed over much of the country, meeting a variety of people. As providers of both news and entertainment, the traveling actors were generally well received in the villages, and they provided entertainment for both the gentry and the commoners. Since he traveled mostly on foot, often alone, Petőfi could often take advantage of the hospitality extended at the farms and manor houses. Thus he came to know a wide spectrum of society, moving easily in all except the aristocratic circles. On these travels he also developed his appreciation for nature, uniting a keen observation with objectivity. What is refreshingly original in his poetry, whether nature poems or portrayals of life, is the lack of sentimentality. The "romantic fallacy" is not found in his poems unless it is used in a consciously metaphoric manner.

Seeing that acting would not provide him a living, Petőfi decided to join the army. He hoped to be stationed near the border of the Austrian dominions and thus "escape" to Switzerland.[4] However, the farthest he got before he was discharged for ill health was Graz. In the months following his discharge he became friends with Mór Jókai, later a prominent novelist but now a student at Pápa. Petőfi was determined to complete his studies and attended classes there. He also joined the literary society and gained recognition as a poet: "A borozó" ("The Wine Drinker"), his first published poem, appeared in the prestigious *Athenaeum* in May, 1842. The same year he won the Society's annual festival with the prize of two gold pieces—to which Count Eszterházy added a third, so pleased was he with the young man's talent.[5]

Petőfi, now nineteen, considered himself a poet; he was determined that this would be his vocation. He planned to finish his studies, become a professional man able to support himself and to help his parents, and pursue his chief love, poetry, at his leisure. Only when a promised position as tutor fell through did he resign himself bitterly to becoming an actor, as he wrote to a school friend, Szeberényi: "Fate pursues me relentlessly. . . . I can't do otherwise. . . . I must become an actor; I must and there is no recourse."[6] But he did reaffirm his goal of becoming a poet. The literary and political situations of the early nineteenth century were particularly favorable to the development of Petőfi's poetic talent, and the circumstances of his life, for all their hardships, also seemed to favor this.

II *The Literary Scene*

First, the two great intellectual movements of the eighteenth century, the Enlightenment and preromanticism, had by this time been interpreted by Hungarian poets and thinkers, and many of the liberal ideas had become part of the life of the middle classes. Second, though close enough to the *nép* (loosely translated as "folk" or "common people," "populace"), Petőfi, by virtue of his education and talents, moved among the intellectual elite of his day, taking his place naturally among the young writers of the capital. His poetical heritage, as well as his political convictions, were shaped by both movements. Finally romanticism, the dominant style in his youth and early career, needed the infusion of new, more realistic, and more positive elements, and Petőfi seemed to provide precisely this.

The Enlightenment entered Hungary through the activity of a group of noble youths, members of the guard of Empress Maria Theresa.[7] Their leader, György Bessenyei (1747–1811), began to mold Hungarian versification to conform to classical models. The quantitative meter suited the language in spite of an inner contradiction, for though there is a definite pattern of long and short syllables, the natural stresses of the language do not always conform to these. Bessenyei's metrical innovations, as well as the linguistic revival, were continued by others, notably Berzsenyi and Vörösmarty for the former and Ferenc Kazinczy for the latter.

But, concurrently with this concern for moving Hungary into the mainstream of Western European literary life, a group of the landed gentry championed the more ancient forms. József Gvadányi (1725–1801) wrote a long humorous narrative in support of old customs against the new ones. Through the description of the adventures of a village official, he ridiculed the French and German customs of the capital. Petőfi, who appreciated Gvadányi's support of native versification, was to attack the influx of foreign fashions in his own time in a poem dedicated to his predecessor.

Literature in this period was in the hands of the nobility. Most of the writers owned land and were thus independent: some were wealthy aristocrats more at home in European courts than in Hungary, yet at this time the interest in Hungarian literature and history gave several of these "amateurs" considerable status. Many of the poets, also, were imprisoned for years after the failure of the Martinovics revolt which had attempted to reestablish some of the independence of the Hungarian kingdom. Ironically, they had acted on the principles of the Enlightenment against a regime that was to become more and more conservative.

The nobility thus became the representative of progressive ideas, especially during the reign of Francis I who placed high tarriffs on books and journals and closed libraries. However, it was also a time of economic gains for the petty nobility who often did not have significant estates but were reasonably well educated and frequently became professionals.

Thus the later eighteenth and early nineteenth centuries were generally favorable for literature. Interest in the revival and development of the Hungarian language was considerable on all levels. It had definite political overtones, and had certainly been spurred by the efforts of Joseph II to make German the administrative and universal language of his Empire. Though some conservatives clung to the Latin tradition, most men realized the need for a viable national language if Hungary were to retain her independent identity. Consequently, Ferenc Széchenyi, one of the richest magnates and himself an author, deeded his library to the nation in 1802. This was to be the foundation of the National Museum. His son, István, was to establish the Academy in 1824, offering one year's income for this cause.

In the intervening years a Hungarian newspaper (1806) was founded, the Transylvanian Museum was established (1814), Hungarian theaters and theatrical companies were formed. At Kolozsvár (Cluj) the first permanent theater presented Körner's *Zriny*. The publication of *Aurora*, a yearbook by Károly Kisfaludi and his group, established the first literary circle centered in Pest and dependent on the public rather than patronage.

One of the most important figures of the linguistic revival was Ferenc Kazinczy, a critic and literary dictator who sought to establish a simple and dignified style and to develop a language capable of being shaped to this classical mold. He, too, had spent months in Kufstein, and upon his release was more dedicated than before to the needs of a "Magyar" culture.

While Kazinczy was a disciple of the Enlightenment in politics and neoclassicism in the arts, Dániel Berzsenyi (1776–1836) was a representative of the values of the earlier aristocratic literature and of preromanticism. A poet of mutability, he wrote in ancient Hungarian meters and used imagery suggestive of strength. The combination gives his poems a forcefulness seldom associated with the theme of eternal change in human life.

Mihály Csokonai Vitéz (1773–1805), a truly important poet of the era, combined baroque and rococo styles with popular (*népi*) culture. He was one of the early students of native Hungarian versification and both his preromantic and popular styles influenced Petőfi's own poetic development. He is perhaps most important for blending the plain speech of his rural subjects with rococo gracefulness.

Finally, Ferenc Kölcsey (1790–1837), whose "Hymnus" was to become the Hungarian national anthem, represented the type of patriotic literature that Petőfi could both imitate and develop. Though thoroughly cosmopolitan, Kölcsey raised patriotism to religious heights. The goal of all noble men became, for him, service of the country. Yet, his patriotism was not blind. Unlike many of his contemporaries, he refused to accept a work without criticism simply because it praised Hungarians, and he was no less sparing in rebuking what he considered bad qualities in Hungarian life.

The dominance of individuals, which had characterized the early decades of the century, gave way to the influence of journals after 1822. The *Aurora* was definitely aimed at women and the literate population of the cities, indicating the end of the dominance of the county nobility. Literary life was increasingly centered in Pest so that this city became the cultural as well as the commercial capital, though the diet continued to meet at Pozsony (Bratislava).

The group of poets associated with the *Aurora* represented a completely new direction from Kazinczy. Károly Kisfaludi (1788–1830) was the central figure. A dramatist who wrote robber dramas in Hungarian historical settings, he was popular and famous. As a poet, some of his folksongs captured the tone and language of the originals even when the subjects were suited to the sophistication of his readers. József Bajza, a good critic but poor poet, and Schedel-Toldy, the literary historian who was instrumental in turning the German-speaking population to Hungarian rather than German literature, were important members of the staff of the *Aurora* as was Mihály Vörösmarty, the most gifted poet of the group.

By the time Petőfi emerged as a poet, the battle between the *Aurora* and Kazinczy and Schedel-Toldy and the Pyrker group had been settled in favor of the Aurora Circle. Hungarian literature was henceforth dependent on the leisured city dweller and the daughters and wives of rural officials. It ceased to be aristocratic though it was still dominated by the lower nobility or "gentry."

The problem of German culture in Hungary thus also had to be faced. In the eighteenth century, many cities and certain regions retained a distinctly German culture even when they identified with Hungary politically and culturally. As intermediaries of German influences, their role was important. Furthermore, as a bourgeois culture, their journals and theaters provided a model (and later, facilities) for Magyar efforts along these lines. The danger came only when the German-language writers began to serve the nationalistic aims of the Habsburg monarchy rather than the interests of the Hungarian nation to which they belonged. Their collections of poems, tales, and historical narratives, as well as the fact that these were published in German,[8] were a plus for Hungarian literature, and by the 1830s they had to become "Magyarized" in order to enter the mainstream of literature and to avoid being merely a provincial literature.

In 1836 the Kisfaludi Társaság was formed to cultivate elite literature and the following year the *Aurora* became the *Athenaeum*, the journal of the society, with Mihály Vörösmarty, József Bajza, and Miklós Toldy as the editors. Unlike its predecessor, this was a periodical devoted to belles lettres and appearing two (later three) times a week. It was soon joined by other publications, most of them devoted to gossip, fashion, news, and literature. The rivalry among these papers provided income for many journalists and poets, but seldom enough to live on. Of the writers of the day perhaps Petőfi was the only one dependent solely on his pen for a living.

III *From Actor to Poet*

When Petőfi first became interested in acting and the theater, Hungarian drama was in its infancy. Most of the dramas were German robber dramas translated or possibly rewritten for Hungarian audiences. Even native Hungarian dramatists wrote in this vein. The best play of the period, *Bánk Bán* by József Katona, was not performed until 1833—twelve years after it appeared as a book. Censorship was chiefly responsible for this, and also for the fact that the first performance was in Kassa (Kosice). This was followed by one in Kolozsvár (Cluj, 1834), and finally in 1839, by the National Theater in Pest, two years after the establishment of this company as a permanent theater in the city which was to become the center of Hungarian cultural life. Though he had been an extra and stagehand at this theater in March and April, 1839, Petőfi could find no steady position. He joined several touring companies, and sought work such as copying reports of the diet (April–June, 1843) or translating. He was becoming known in the literary and intellectual circles as a "young man with promise," but was still penniless and unknown when the dissolution of the acting group he had joined, and his own illness, left him stranded in Debrecen for the winter of 1843–1844. He had been writing poetry all along, and now he decided to hazard all on that. Throughout the winter he polished and arranged the verses, copying the final version into a home-made notebook. In February he set out for Pest, determined to submit the 108 poems to Mihály Vörösmarty. If the elder poet approved them, Petőfi decided he would remain a poet and somehow earn his living by his pen; if not, he would give up poetry forever. Petőfi tended to make extreme decisions, but then his circumstances were extreme. The venture succeeded, and this volume, *Versek 1842–1844* (*Poems*) firmly established his reputation.

Mihály Vörösmarty, the most prestigious member of the Kisfaludi Társaság as well as one of the editors of the *Athenaeum*, was regarded as the poet laureate of Hungary. He had made his name with a series of historical narratives, of which the epic on the conquest of Hungary by the seven Magyar tribes under Árpád, *Zalán futása* (1824–1825; *The Flight of Zalán*) was the most popular. In the 1830s he turned to patriotic themes after a brief period of writing melancholy philosophical poetry, but he emphasized heroism and humanism rather than narrow patriotism. Death, even the death of the nation, is a frequent theme, but in this preoccupation Vörösmarty was not alone. As will be seen later, even Petőfi shared the cyclic view of nations and cultures on which this theory of the death of nations is based.

Having borrowed money from a friend to pay his debt to the widow who had given him food and lodging over the winter, Petőfi started walking the 130 miles with hardly more than a few forints, a knapsack, and a large staff to be used both as an aid on the muddy roads and for protection. All of these were gifts of the students of the academy at Debrecen. Later, traveling the same roads, he was to write:

> I traveled all alone here on the Hegyalja; I did not meet with a soul, a living thing. Every man sought shelter since it was terrible weather. The whistling wind sprinkled sleeting rain on me. It was coming straight at my face. The tears, which the coldness of the rain and my general misery caused to flow, froze on my face. . . . I thought: "if I can sell them [the poems], good; if I cannot sell them, that is good also; then I will either starve or die of cold and all sufferings will be at end."[9]

Even so, when he stopped at Eger, the welcome given him by the seminarians inspired one of his drinking songs, "Egri hangok" ("Sounds of Eger"). Happiness and joy of camaraderie are only muted by the remembrance of lost national glory, not personal griefs. The hardships of the poet's life stamped his work, yet he refused to yield to melancholy or self-pity. A realist rather than a romantic in this, he decided to face the worst but seldom brooded over disappointments. Therefore, though his experiences provided the material for his poetry, they did not darken the psychology of the poems.

The gamble paid off, and even before the poems could be published, the Nemzeti Kör, a literary and cultural society devoted to nationalistic (i.e., Magyar, not Austrian) causes, started a subscription for him. He was also invited to become assistant editor of the literary and fashion journal *Pesti Divatlap* (*Fashion Magazine of Pest*). In addition, he could sell his poems to this and other journals. His future thus somewhat assured, Petőfi paid a long visit to his parents.

István Petrovics held the lease on the inn and butcher shop at Dunavecse, and Sándor now made a point of ascertaining his father's feelings and also letting everyone know that he was a man with a job and some means.[10] In short, he wanted to prove to his father and to his father's friends, that he was a son to be proud of: he was known and appreciated in Pest, and wanted his father's blessing and recognition, too. And the old man, who never could recover either financially or emotionally from the ruin brought on him as a result of a bad investment and a severe flooding of the Danube, came to respect the young genius he never could understand. The poems about his parents, to be discussed later, show the closeness of father and son in these later years.

The months spent at Dunavecse had their effect in a series of personal poems; they also contributed to the development of Petőfi's style. From this time on he made more frequent use of the simple and ingenuous style of the folksongs, making it his most characteristic genre, adapting its meter and language, its imagery and "philosophy" to a variety of songs, lyrics, odes, and narratives, as well as to a variety of subjects. From this time his poems also became more personal, though the lives of the peasants continued to furnish many of his materials and images. The visit gave him a chance to reassess his priorities and to turn even more consciously from artificial and imitative forms. Vörösmarty had been impressed by his sincerity and directness. Petőfi had already seemed like a breath of fresh air from the Great Hungarian Plain, but now he made directness and sincerity a real program.

IV *Romanticism and Liberal Ideas*

1844 marked the beginning of Petőfi's career as a poet and reformer, publicist and politician. From the time he assumed his duties with the *Pesti Divatlap* on July 1 until he died in one of the last battles of the Revolution on August 29, 1849, he was a public personality who influenced events more than he or others realized. But to fully appreciate his position, it is necessary to know something of the literary, social, and political life of Hungary in the Reform era and the years leading to the Revolution.

The Reform era, generally defined as the years between 1825 and 1848, was characterized by the demands of liberals to implement reforms in the entire machinery of imperial government. Foremost among these, and dating back to the 1790s, was the insistence on the wider use of Hungarian. This awareness of the need for a national language had already led to the linguistic and literary revival discussed earlier. Social and economic reforms were seen by many as equally important, though more difficult to obtain. Suggestions for the extension of taxation to the nobility and the establishment of a capitalistic economy were met with opposition not only from the court, but also from many of the Hungarian nobles who were reluctant to yield their privileges. Still, the atmosphere of change was created, and statesmen of the stature of Count István Széchenyi and Lajos Kossuth emerged. Poets and writers supported these men and the reforms they advocated, from the abolition of the vestiges of feudalism to the creation of a democratic republic. The consensus, however, was in favor of a constitutional monarchy (on the much-admired English model), a capitalistic economy, and a national policy that actively supported the use of the native language in all areas of life. Petőfi was attracted to the more radical programs, such as the abolition of the privileges of birth and wealth and the establishment of a uniform legal and political system, and these views were shared by many. Even the abolition of the monarchy (a distinctly separate question from the revocation of the hereditary right of the Habsburgs to the Hungarian crown) was debated by the liberal politicians of the day.

Hungarian romanticism was thus characterized by a positive spirit asosciated with the Enlightenment elsewhere. For example, Mihály Vörösmarty, Ferenc Kölcsey, and József Eötvös, the prominent writers of the 1820s and 1830s chose Johann Wolfgang von Goethe, Friedrick Schiller, and Victor Hugo as models, thus identifying themselves with the doers of the romantic period, rather than the dreamers. Naturally, the interest in national history which was an aspect of romanticism in England and especially Germany, became an important characteristic of Hungarian romanticism also. This common interest united the romantics and the writers of the Reform era. István Sőtér noted that romanticism was the "literary expression of the spirit of the liberal nobility," which eventually led to the "nationalistic folk poetry of the plebian-democratic attitudes of Petőfi and Arany."[11] Sőtér summarized the stages of this development as follows: (1) Up to 1817, the preparatory stage, was marked by the resistance of the nobility to the continued encroachment of the Habsburg government of Hungarian rights; (2) 1817–1837 marked a period of gains that culminated in the opening of the Hungarian National Theater in Pest in 1837; (3) 1841–1845 saw the emergence of liberal causes and more politicized literary activity; (4) 1845–1848 was the period of Petőfi's most important activity and of his emergence as one of the leaders of the younger generation of Hungarian writers; (5) after 1849, romanticism gradually gave way to realism or, as in the case of the novelist Mór Jókai, sought compromises with it.[12]

Each of these periods had an impact on the development of Hungarian romanticism, and thus also on Petőfi. The patriotic concerns of the "noble" literature of the early part of the century can be seen in some of his romances as well as in numerous poems; the liberal, even populist concerns of the 1830s leads even more directly to Petőfi's folk and folk-oriented poetry. Thus, by being concerned with contemporary problems, even when these were clothed in historical garb, the poets moved toward the acceptance of realism rather than the rejection of it often associated with romanticism. Petőfi consciously embraced this movement; he believed that the poet's mission was to teach, specifically to serve the cause of national renewal and personal freedom through his poetry. Though more successful and better recognized than most, Petőfi was not alone in this interpretation of the poet's mission. Kölcsey, Vörösmarty, and others shared in this dedication.

The optimism of the Reform era was a result of the belief that literature had a goal beyond itself. The poets of the 1820s and 1830s had, in a way, prepared the ground for the Revolution of 1848. Their ideas had become part of the consciousness of the new generation, although they were by no means the only mentors. Both French ideas and the example of the Young Germany movement were important. Petőfi read several histories of the French Revolution, which he considered a model (albeit with reservations) for radical reform. He admired the popular poet Béranger, from whom he translated several poems. But these liberal ideals received a special development in his works, because Petőfi was aware that in Hungary's case the political reformers had to be concerned not only with encouraging popular values and traditions as a means of reaching the common man, but that they also had to revive these native traditions to counteract foreign influences. What emerged was a popular national literature in contrast to the earlier aristocratic and the later bourgeois literature.

Similarly, the ideal of liberty contained a duality not associated with it in France or Germany: it involved both the goals of national independence from Habsburg rule and personal liberty, namely, the extension of equality to the entire population regardless of birth. Though one or the other goal would predominate at a certain time, the two could not be separated. Petőfi supported both, though universal liberty was his more immediate concern. On the other hand, the nobility renounced its privileges for the sake of universal freedom. As Antal Szerb aptly expressed it, "the Hungarian liberty [ideal] cannot be understood through its logical components—it is so thoroughly emotional in its character and it is such a thorough blending of the finitism of the race, of ancient and basic desires for independence in the region of ideals, that it can be comprehended only as an emotional fact and only through the enthusiasm of the chosen poets."[13] Petőfi was one such poet.

The literary life of the 1830s and 1840s was hardly monolithic. Three well-defined groups waged an often bitter war of words. The first, comprised mostly of the elite, aristocratic authors such as the novelists József Eötvös and Zsigmond Kemény, János Erdélyi, an important critic, and Ferenc Pulszky,who was to be a popularizer of Hungarian literature in England, continued the romantic traditions of the previous era, particularly in intellectual novels. A second group, labeled the "literary proletariat" (mostly minor talents who supplied the journals with provocative material), united against both the Aurora authors and the third group, loosely identified as the "radical" poets and the Young Hungary group, including not only Petőfi, Jókai, and Arany, but also Mihály Tompa, Pál Gyulai, the Vahot brothers, and many others who were to be a part of the Revolution and who proved to be the representatives of the new literary era. All of them were poor and dependent to some degree on their writings. Their chief outlets were the fashion magazines, which sought poetry to fill their literary sections. The *Pesti Divatlap,* on which Petőfi had his first steady literary position, was the oldest of these journals. Later, Petőfi left this journal because of personal conflicts and went to work for the *Életképek* (*Panorama*), the chief rival of the *Divatlap.* The conservative, aristocratic *Honderű* (*Serenity of the Homeland*) provided a forum for Petőfi's rivals who often attacked both the style and the content of his poetry.

In the atmosphere of literary revival that characterized Hungarian intellectual life at that time, it was natural that men of letters should turn to the prominent figures of European romanticism as well as to the political and philosophical heritage of the Enlightenment. Thus, Petőfi was familiar with the works of Schiller and Goethe, Shelley and Byron, Hugo and Lamartine, as well as such lesser yet popular poets as Moore and Béranger. Above all, he admired Shakespeare and not only translated his *Coriolanus* but also urged János Arany to undertake some of the dramas. The complete translation of Shakespeare, though not finished until the early years of this century, owes much to his vision and original enthusiasm.

As a student, and in the early years of his career, Petőfi was definitely influenced by the tastes and preoccupations of the time, although he already showed independence in choosing popular, rather than the fashionable poetic diction of the day. He made the folksong the foundation of his style with the result that he "was able to raise every subject to the level of poetry."[14] At the same time, he was a realist who took his inspiration from his own life and the scenes around him. The visit home in the spring of 1844 firmly established these priorities. From this time on few poems lack the healthy realism of the folksong, or its lyricism and simplicity of language. In the next four years he was to create a truly native lyrical style which, though influenced by European fashions and models, was not closely imitative of them; it is this style that he left as a legacy to later poets.

V *In the Public Eye*

Having accepted the position of assistant editor at the *Pesti Divatlap* as of July 1, 1844, Petőfi became a well-known figure in Pest. His two long poems, *A helység kalapácsa* (*The Hammer of the Village*) and *János Vitéz*, as well as *Versek 1842–1844* (*Poems*) appeared in quick succession. These were followed by the cycle of elegaic poems, *Cipruslombok Etelke sírjáról* (*Cypress Leaves from the Tomb of Etelke*). In March, 1845, he left the *Divatlap*, and, never having seen the northern tier of Hungary, set out for this region of the Northern Carpathian mountains. The record of his journey, "Travel Notes," was published in *Életképek*, the rival journal.

The rest of that year, and most of the following, brought little success. His drama, *Zöld Marci*, was not accepted by the National Theater and his proposal to the wealthy Bertha Mednyánszky was refused; the poetic record of his love, *Szerelem gyöngyei* (*The Pearls of Love*), appeared in October and in the following month the second volume of his poems was published. But these brought little income, and he lived either at home or with friends while he worked to increase the remuneration given authors for their writings. To this end he formed the Society of Ten (Tízek Társasága) and led a brief strike against the publishers. The only concrete result seemed to have been Petőfi's closer attachment to Frankenburg's *Életképek*, since Frankenburg offered better prices than did other publishers.

This time was also one of increasing recognition for Petőfi. He was beginning to be known abroad, and had good connections with many of the prominent Hungarian authors. In fact, the limited success of the writer's strike was partly due to his recognized position as leader of the radical poets. While his second drama, *Tigris és hiéna* (*Tiger and Hyena*) was not scheduled for performance during the regular season, his novel *A hóhér kötele* (*The Hangman's Rope*), and *Felhők* (*Clouds*), a cycle of philosophical poems, continued to keep him before the public. This last volume of poetry showed the versatility he was capable of, and in August, 1846, he signed a contract with the publisher and bookseller, Gustáv Emich, for his *Collected Poems*. This was to assure him a modest yet certain annual income.

A trip to the county of Szatmár, planned as a prelude to a visit to Transylvania, brought the most notable turn of events in his life so far: he met, and fell in love with, Júlia Szendrey, the daughter of the manager of Count Károlyi's estates in eastern Hungary and, by birth and education, a member of the upper classes. Her father, who is immortalized as an irascible bigot in Petőfi's poetry, was a conservative local functionary, a member of the petty nobility, and a fairly typical father who wanted social and financial security for his daughter. Júlia was a romantic young girl, rather headstrong and unconventional, intrigued by the fashionable liberal ideas of 1846, and certainly by the young poet who represented them so well.

Petőfi by now (September, 1846) had become a well-known poet and was even more popular as the leader of the more revolutionary group of Hungarian authors. Though still within the liberal camp, they represented the "left" which sought social as well as political reforms. These ideas were embodied in their writings which concerned common topics and were written in plain language. In the two days that he had been in Nagykároly, Petőfi had already drawn attention to himself by his criticism of Count Károlyi. He had also become friends with the liberal Count Teleki. Under the circumstances, it is not surprising that Júlia wrote to her friend, Mária Terey:

> That Petőfi is a wicked boy: he can look at one with so much passion. . . . P. will be in Károly again for the elections. If you only knew how glad I am in anticipation of this time. Truly, if I did not know myself better, I would believe I am in L——! But I console myself that it will pass. Still, I shudder when I think that it is not beyond the bounds of possibility that a serious, lasting feeling will follow—Oh! he is a poet![15]

On his side, Petőfi seemed to have fallen in love with Júlia just as suddenly. He proposed and, bowing to her father's opposition, agreed to wait the year stipulated for a final answer. The poems of these months reflect their often stormy courtship, but also form a record of the deepening of the poet's attachment as he made of Júlia the idol in whom was united all that the poet held dear. Whatever she might have been in reality, it is this picture that has to be accepted; she never seems to have disappointed him. Now that he had serious plans for marriage, Petőfi sought to create a more secure financial basis for himself. He became a regular contributor to the *Életképek* in November, 1846, and in January of the next year he published his drama *Tigris és hiéna*. In March, his *Összes költeményei* (*Collected Poems*) appeared. A second trip to Szatmár followed, and on May 26 he proposed again to Júlia; the wedding date was set for September.

Before returning to Pest, Petőfi spent ten days with his friend and fellow poet, János Arany, at Nagyszalonta. The two had been friends since February of that year when Petőfi wrote a poem in praise of Arany and his poem, *Toldi*, an epic based on a hero of fifteenth-century Hungary. This visit deepened their friendship, and led to a very fruitful cooperation between the two men.

Still restless, Petőfi made a second journey to the mountains, this time traveling in the more easterly regions of the Northern Carpathians. He thus became familiar with almost all of the regions of Hungary; he knew them more closely than many a casual traveler. He studied both the scenery and the customs, and sent his observations to a periodical in Budapest for publication. Under the title, "Úti levelek Kerényi Frigyeshez" ("Travel Notes to Frigyes Kerényi"), they began appearing in *Hazánk* (*Our Homeland*) starting in late August and running for nineteen installments. One of the most interesting segments is that which gives an account of his wedding, honeymoon, and return to Pest after a trip to Kolozsvár. Written in a conversational, almost colloquial manner, they reflect the poet's personality without affectation. But these letters also show the esteem he enjoyed at the time, particularly among the younger generation. For example, Count Teleki lent his castle of Kotló for the honeymoon, leaving only the cook to look after them, and in Kolozsvár the Transylvanian youth gave them a torchlight welcome. This naturally pleased Petőfi, because he could let his wife see that he *was* important and respected, even if not in her parents' circle.

Petőfi and his wife moved into their lodgings in Pest in November, 1847. They were, from the first, active in the social life of the young radical poets. Since Júlia shared her husband's sentiments, their home was frequently the scene of political meetings and heated discussions on the shape reform should take. The winter of 1847–1848 brought more political activity to the city, and Petőfi felt obliged to take an active part, even to help direct events. After all, he had made part of his reputation on his political views; he had been sincere, moreover, in stating that the poet's task is both to inspire the people and to take an active part in leading them. Thus, much of what he wrote at this time was politically motivated.

On the other hand, he also felt it imperative to ensure a steady income, and so he wrote for publication as well. Since Petőfi had always written systematically, devoting several hours daily to his poetry, the two interests did not affect his productivity. Moreover, these two interests coincided. Thus, while he contributed to many journals, the *Életképek* and *Hazám* were eager customers even for political poems. The latter was especially important for the more liberal poems: it was located in Győr, not Pest, and the censor here was much more permissive. The authorities did not expect inflammatory materials in a journal that had originally been called *Vaterland*, and which was supported by ethnic German citizens. Finally, he seldom needed to revise, although he did make some changes and always prepared a clean copy before submitting a poem for consideration to a publisher. This helps account for the amazing volume of his work in spite of his short life and the often adverse conditions under which he wrote.

Though neither Buda nor Pest was the political capital, Pest was the center of the opposition party and of the young radical leaders who demanded the liberalization of society. It was, more importantly, the artistic and intellectual center, and there was considerable sentiment even among conservatives that the capital should be returned to Buda, and that a parliamentary form of government should replace the semifeudal diet and royal council. Social, legal, and economic reforms were sought. As a wave of revolution spread over Europe, men such as the Counts Széchenyi and Batthyány, and Louis Kossuth, also pressed for reforms. Petőfi, as a leader of the radicals, would have preferred independence from the Habsburgs and the establishment of a republic, though at first he was willing to accept less sweeping programs.

On March 14, the eve of what he suspected might be a major demonstration for greater responsiveness from the government to the needs of the people, Petőfi wrote his "Nemzeti Dal" ("National Ode"). The next day, through a series of negotiations backed up by demonstrations, he and the liberal youth of the city, most of them his friends, won the acceptance in principle of their program of reform, effected freedom of the press by printing both the "National Ode" and the "Twelve Points" without requesting the censor's approval, and freed Mihály Táncsics, a political prisoner in Buda who had been incarcerated on the freedom of the press issue.[16] The Revolution—as yet a peaceful internal Reform—had begun.

Petőfi continued his involvement in events from this time on. When both the public safety and national security seemed threatened by the invasions of Jellačić and similar guerrilla bands, he became a member of the National Guard (i.e., "Nemzetőr" which he was to commemorate in one of his poems). He joined the staff of the *Életképek*, which had been edited by his friend Mór Jókai since April, 1848. He published his diary on the events of March–April, 1848, a lively if fragmented account of his activities and thoughts in these days, and also the translation of *Coriolanus*. In September, he undertook a recruiting tour, and by October 16 he joined the regular army. The War of Independence was in full force now, relations between the Hungarians and the Hapsburgs having broken down completely; even the fact that Julia was expecting their first child in December did not allow him to draw back from the struggle he had so often sought in his poems.

Petőfi's career in the army was full of problems. Never one to accept authority easily and without questions, he clashed over matters of etiquette and protocol. But with General Bem, a Polish patriot who had come to help the Hungarians after the defeat of the Polish uprising, there were no problems. Petőfi joined Bem's army in January, 1849, and—except for a brief period when personal attacks forced him to resign his commission—remained in his service until his death. Through most of the year Petőfi participated in the Transylvanian campaigns, visiting his wife and son whenever a lull in the fighting or his adjutant's duties allowed. On July 31, 1849, he took part in the Battle of Segesvár and was killed by Cossack forces of the Russian army which had come to aid the Austrians according to the agreements of the Holy Alliance. Petőfi's body was never found, since he was buried, according to eye witnesses, in a mass grave. However, this was not known until much later, and many rumors of his living on in exile, in hiding, or in a Siberian labor camp were circulated in the 1850s as proof of the people's reluctance to accept his death. His widow's remarriage was severely criticized, though eventually the poet's death had to be accepted. His poetry, however, continued to live on.[17]

CHAPTER 2

Early Poems

I *Seeking a Personal Style*

PETŐFI considered few poems written before 1842 worthy of inclusion among his published works. This date, therefore, can be taken as the true beginning of his poetic career and the end of his apprenticeship. Earlier he had been an imitator of Mihály Vörösmarty and József Bajza among Hungarian poets, Friedrich Schiller, Heinrich Heine, and Nicholaus Lenau among the Germans, and finally, of the Latin poet Horace whose works he had studied with considerable interest in school. The influence of these poets is most marked in the early poems. A flirtation with sentimentality and exoticism is noticeable, as is a tendency toward dreamy melancholy. On the positive side, there are hints of a masculine perseverance and a dedication to an ideal which attest to his admiration of Schiller. Horace seems to have bequeathed a sense of decorum and classical restraint as well as an appreciation for simple, rural pleasures as a suitable subject for poetry: some of Petőfi's genre scenes are very close to Horace's eclogues in their spirit. In later years, the influence of these poets became less and less noticeable, although it continued to enrich his work. As he became more independent and more sure of himself, he experimented with adapting both their styles and their ideas to his own poetic needs.

Already in the first poem published under the name of Petőfi—the one he placed at the head of the collection he carried to Vörösmarty in 1844[1]—"Hazámban" ("In My Homeland"), this process is evident. In its style, the poem is conventional. The folksong had been popular since the days of Károly Kisfaludi a dozen years earlier and Petőfi used the most widely imitated form, namely, the four-stress line with *a a b b* rhyme. Further, the poem used more archaic and poetic words than would be found in Petőfi's later poetry, so that it did not have the impression of simple speech made poetic by the aptness of expression, the originality of imagery, and the musical quality of words which was made famous in his more mature poems. What identified it as a product of the mature poet was its depth of feeling, evident in spite of the conventional images, and the handling of the musical qualities of verse to have them reflect the meaning.

In later poems, Petőfi developed a verse form based on authentic folksongs, early Hungarian poetry, and the patterns of Hungarian speech. He knew that much of Hungarian prosody had been based on Latin and German models, and urged that these "rules" be reexamined for their validity. He did not ignore the classical and the Western European influences, but neither did he reject the speech or the poetry of the common man simply because these were considered vulgar or uncultured. Keenly aware of the pervasive influence of German on the Hungarian language, and of its impact even on those who sought to purify and revitalize Hungarian, he was convinced that only by listening to the people could the task of "Magyarizing" Hungarian poetry be successful.[2]

Years after Petőfi's death, János Arany, by then a respected literary critic and the president of the Hungarian Academy, defined the "Hungarian national meter" chiefly on the basis of a study of Petőfi's use of native rhythms.[3] These, he concluded, were the same as could be found in the poetry of the sixteenth and the seventeenth centuries and in the hymns of an earlier age.

On the basis of these studies Arany came to the conclusion that the lines of Hungarian poetry are made up of bars analogous to bars of music. This reflects the close connection to folksong. Each measure (or bar), Arany determined, is made up of two to four syllables; this number, while often consistent, is not as rigid as the number of syllables in classical verse. A poem can be made up of lines of an odd or an even number of syllables; it can even have a varied number of syllables per line. Alternating long and short lines, for example, are possible without a radical change in the pattern. However, the stresses, determined by the rhythms of the language, generally fall on the first syllable. Thus, a pattern is established. The effect is often reminiscent of dactylic and trochaic meters. However, variation is possible both in the placement of the stress and in the determination of the syllables per measure so that no one foot need predominate.[4] In fact, some of the alliterative four-stress lines in Petőfi's early work often resemble Anglo-Saxon or Middle English verse.

The line is named for the predominant number of syllables, although the type of measure used is important. A regular line, for example, consists of one strong and one weak stress divided among four syllables. The classic line is the divided eights, so named because a strong caesura divides the line. The "sevens," the "sixes," and the "fives" each have only one full measure, generally the first one. The second half of the line thus has only one stressed syllable and two, one, or no unstressed ones. The effect allows great flexibility: the "fives" pattern is a short masculine line whereas the "sevens" is a longer feminine one.[5]

Lines based on the eight pattern are "regular"; those based on the twelves or three measures per line are "quick." The basic line in this category is often called the "three-part twelve" to indicate the triple construction of the line. Lines of eleven, ten and nine syllables are common. As with the "regular" lines, here, too, the truncated measures tend to come at the end of the line, giving these a feminine effect. With this pattern, the third measure, whether full or truncated, is often dropped as a half line. Petőfi used these "tags" for many effects: humor, emphasis, refrains, and so on.

Rhyme, the other element of versification, was used by Petőfi in 798 poems out of his 856.[6] The *a b c b* pattern is used in almost half of the poems; the remainder, however, exploit the full range of possibilities: the couplet, the *a b a b* and the *a b b a* quatrain, and the pattern most often found in older Hungarian poetry, *a a b b*. Longer stanzas show similar variety: *a b a b c c*, *a a b c b a*, *a a b b c d c d*, *a b a b c c d d*, *a a b c c b*, and so on. Generally, Petőfi used the half-rhyme and the couplet in poems that had Hungarian rhythms and the more complicated rhyme schemes in the quantitative poems. Terza rima and various triplet rhymes, sometimes headed or concluded by an unrhymed line, are other patterns he occasionally used.[7] In the unrhymed poems both assonance and an occasional rhyme served to call attention to key words or to provide humor.

The rules of versification summarized above had not been

studied or established when Petőfi began writing. He seemed to use them instinctively, following the pattern he detected in the folksongs as well as in the works of poets of the sixteenth and seventeenth centuries: Sebestyén Tinódi Lantos, who, like a medieval minstrel or balladeer, had recorded the events of the Turkish wars in verse, and Miklós Zrinyi, the author of an epic based on these wars. He defended with his characteristic conviction the validity of his choices against charges that such practices led to formless, irregular verses. Eventually, both he and his public were vindicated: he is the acknowledged founder of the modern lyrical style.

II *The Lyrics of 1842–1844*

In the first period of Petőfi's poetic development, the folksong and older Hungarian poetry had a strong influence on him. His style tended to be playful, and he was aware of his audience even when writing personal lyrics. His landscape poems and folksongs both created dramatic scenes: he changed the static descriptive poetry of the eighteenth century into an immediate, personal expression with which his readers could identify. The same talent for sensing what was appropriate as well as poetically successful allowed him to vary the patterns discussed above without becoming formless. This is one of the marks of his talent, but it was also what made him immediately popular, even before critics were ready to accept his innovations.

In 1842–1844 Petőfi wrote primarily in the folksong style, though the subjects ranged from anacreontics to love lyrics to personal and meditative poems. In "A borozó" ("The Wine Drinker") he touched on a theme he was to use again and again: problems and trials are forgotten when he is drinking, and neither fate, nor malicious men, nor flirtatious girls can bother him. In the numerous "wine songs" he was to write he used a well-established tradition of both classical and Hungarian literature to direct attention to problems, conditions, or attitudes he wanted to comment on. Other poems reflect the life of the village and the plain. In "Hortobágyi kocsmárosné" ("Tavern Hostess of the Hortobágy") the speaker calls for a bottle of wine to warm himself after the long trip from Debrecen to the Hortobágy—the wild winds whistle, but a glance from the blue eyes of the mistress of the inn will surely warm him. A similarly carefree attitude is portrayed in "A faluban utcahosszat" ("The Length of the Village Street"), in which a young man who had been rejected by his lover has the gypsy follow him around with gay tunes lest his former sweetheart suspect that his heart is breaking. This defiant stance is one of the most pervasive in Petőfi's early poems. They reflect his own hard life of wanderings most closely and suggest the escape valve used by him, also, to cope with his personal setbacks and what was often a hopeless situation.

"Egri hangok" ("Sounds of Eger") uses this genre for a more serious purpose. The poem opens with a quiet winter scene: on the ground there is snow; in the skies, clouds; but for the poet everything is fine because he is among friends in a warm room, drinking the fine wines of Eger. The speaker's mood, as shown in the third stanza, is not the rowdiness of earlier poems, but serenity. He paints a scene of happiness and contentment:

Kedvemnek ha magja volna:
Elvetném a hó felett,
S ha kikelne: rozsaerdő
Koszorúzná a telet.
S hogyha földobnám az égre
Szívemet,
Melegítné a világot
Nap helyet![8]

If my good spirits would have seeds: / I'd sow them above the snow, / And when they sprout, a forest of roses / Would crown Winter. / If I would fling to the sky / My heart / It, and not the sun, / Would warm the world.

Having once established this mood and scene, Petőfi skillfully manipulated it to a more serious statement. He moved on to consider the historical associations of the city of Eger, scene of one of the more memorable sieges of the Turkish wars, and through this, the decline of Hungary as a nation. While the melancholy, nostalgic, patriotic poem was popular in the early nineteenth century, positive overtones immediately set this work apart. Furthermore, Petőfi's innovative use of first-person experience in the anacreontic made this a trend-setting piece.

Most of the poems of these years, with the exception of two cycles of love poetry, were folksongs or lyrics in the same style and mood. Petőfi wrote for the readers of the fashionable journals. Even the poems written and revised during the winter of 1843–1844 were in this style. After he signed a contract with the *Pesti Divatlap* and other journals to supply poems on a regular basis, he was under even more pressure to write for the tastes of the public. While the truly great poems were few, surprisingly many were quite good: the content and style were both generally light and playful. Petőfi eschewed poetic hyperbole and the excesses of sentimentality, gently molding public taste to his own more restrained style. He avoided the more serious themes, or at least gave these a light touch. For example, when a poem threatened to become overloaded with emotion, he quickly reverted to the external, objective scene.

The folksong, as it was formed and polished by him, blended form and content. The opening scene was picturesque and generally firmly established a specific natural setting or nature parallel. The natural scene, the comparisons and metaphors harmonized with the established mood, and the ideas followed in logical sequence. Petőfi's poetry is remarkable for the ease with which his ideas are developed, but the logic is often deceptively simple: often novel ideas are sprung on the reader and he is led to accept these as obviously true. Occasionally, there is a change in tone or mood of the poem, but in such cases the natural parallels are also changed and the sequence of ideas remains clear so that the organization of the poem is not marred.

These elements can be illustrated by reference to two early poems, "Árvalányhaj a süvegem bokrétája" ("Feathergrass is the Cockade of My Hat") and "Befordultam a konyhára" ("I Turned into the Kitchen"). Both are love poems, and in both the speaker is a young peasant lad; the scenes and images are the stuff of everyday life. The first compares the speaker's lover to a flower of the *puszta*, i.e., the semiarid regions of the Hungarian Plain. The flower (feathergrass) is called "orphan-maidenhair" in Hungarian, and this gives the poet the opportunity to set up a parallel:

Árvalányhaj a süvegem bokrétája,

Árva leány a szerelmem violája;
Azt magamnak kinn a pusztán szakasztottam,
Ezt magamnak a faluban választottam.

Orphan-maidenhair is the cockade of my hat, / Orphan-maiden is the violet of my love; / That one I picked out there on the *puszta,* / This one I chose here in the village. (104)

In the second stanza, the speaker asserts that the maiden is not only beautiful, but also good. His proof of her goodness is given in a neatly turned simile: the blue flower (cornflower) grows among the pure wheat, and there is a blue flower in her eyes, too. And, since wheat is good and of great value, so is she. The poem is tightly controlled; it is also characteristically built up on nature parallels, so that the lack of logic is completely obscured.

The metrical pattern, the "three-part twelves," is one frequently used in folksong. It allows the poet to divide his lines into three phrases to correspond to the three measures. Each phrase gives an essential part of the thought, and also forces economy of expression.

The second poem is a lively, dramatic description of a young man falling in love: the speaker goes into the kitchen, presumably to light his pipe—but it is already burning. He really goes in because he saw a pretty girl there. She is making a fire, and though the fire blazes, it is nothing to the flaming of her eyes. He goes in, she looks at him: his burning pipe goes out but his sleeping heart is enflamed. Each of these actions is described in one self-contained stanza, so that the stanzaic pattern already corresponds to the content. The metrics also reflect the seeming simplicity of the poem. It is in the very common "divided eights" with a strong and a weaker stress for each of the twice four syllables that give the poem its basic structure. Furthermore, each stanza is divided into two units of two lines linked by rhymes as well as by sense. The interplay of this parallelism and contrast is manipulated for full effect, since the sense of the poem depends on these seeming contradictions.

One of the longer poems in this style, "A virágnak megtiltani nem lehet" ("The Flower Cannot Be Forbidden") also begins with this dualism, but then allows the basic idea—the force of the speaker's love—to take over. Petőfi did not abandon the nature imagery, however; the girl is called "lily-of-the-valley,"[9] an endearment popular because the Hungarian term unites two appropriate metaphors: flower and pearl. His feelings alternate between hope and despair, as do the clouds and the sun on an autumn day, and, finally, he calls on "the star of his happiness," to shine on him to forestall his life's "sad night." The final couplet, "Love me, pearl of my soul, if you may, / So that God may bless your soul," not only recalls the earlier images of luminescence, but seems to bring a serious, almost somber note into the lighthearted lyric. This seriousness is a quality never wholly absent from Petőfi's poetry, although here the progression of the day and of life may have been the justification for the inclusion of the imagery of death. The meter, based on the twelve rather than the eight syllable pattern, also suggests a meditative line: two "eights" followed by a three-syllable measure that contains only one accented syllable and slows the line considerably.

An example of the narrative style, "Fürdik a holdvilág" ("The Moonlight is Bathing"), presents the regrets of an outlaw for the life he has drifted into. The nature parallel is established in opening stanza:

> Fürdik a holdvilág az ég tengerében,
> Mélaz a haramja erdő közepében:
> Sűrű a füvön az éj harmatozása,
> De sűrűbb két szeme könnyének hullása.

The moonlight bathes in the sea of the sky, / The brigand is pensive in the midst of the forest; / Thick is the dew of the evening on the grass, / But even thicker the falling of tears from his eyes. (90)

Then the man speaks, repenting his actions and his failure to listen to his mother's warnings. Only her death, the decay of their home, and the gallows which await him keep him with his robber companions.

The metrical pattern is the "quartered twelves," a relatively slow and measured line often used in narrative poetry. Since each unit of four syllables receives only one strong accent, the stress can depend on the needs of the line. Here, the parallelism of the natural scene and the emotional state of the speaker is handled line by line, and the couplet rhyme reenforces this.

For Petőfi, these years represented experimentation in a variety of forms and genres. They also showed his determination to shun flowery language and empty sentiment. "Lopott ló" ("Stolen horse") is a fast-paced ballad that reports the theft of a horse by a *betyár*[10] who took the steed as recompense for the owner's daughter having stolen his heart! The joke is supported by the short lines that give the poem an appropriate lightness. The three-syllable half line (i.e., one measure), is used for humorous emphasis here as it is in the longer, more complicated poem, "Szeget szeggel" ("Tit for Tat"). The same idea is developed here, but from a different perspective: the poem is a tongue-in-cheek complaint by a young boy who has been thoroughly thrashed by a neighbor for stealing pears—but he will have his revenge when the man next comes to steal kisses from his sister.

The poet's talent for precise observation and his ability to see the humor of situations are clear in his description of the gypsy caravan in "Vándorélet" ("Vagabond Life"). Inspired by a picture of the noted painter Dániel Barabás, the poem gives each of the figures emotions and histories: the ancient nag "has long ago shed his colt's teeth," and spends his days in fasting and mourning. The crying children are equally ill at ease in the saddlebags or walking, and the stolen pig is troublesome, as if suspecting the approaching end.

Another poem, a playful compliment to his favorite older Hungarian poet, József Gvadányi, is Petőfi's vehicle for praising the simple style of his eighteenth-century model. The tone, appropriately, is light, even though Petőfi begins by addressing the long-dead poet with the reminder that "his pen is long since at rest and the grave has long since opened for him." The gist of the poem, however, is an attack on the use of fancy phrases and German constructions, which, in contrast to the honest poetry of Gvadányi, threaten to ruin the mother tongue. What gives the poem its particular charm, however, is Petőfi's use of the archaic language and the alexandrine meter of the older poet.

While the bulk of Petőfi's poetic output was lyrical, the variety in moods and themes is great. Least significant are the love poems of these years; they show no personal commitment and are merely fashionable exercises. More interesting are the poems about his family and friends. They generally exhibit a mastery of form and are full of intense yet controlled feelings. He is always involved in these. "Füstbement terv" ("A Plan Gone up in Smoke") is a soliloquy on how he will greet his mother upon their reunion. The situation is given simply and directly, and the surprise conclusion is realistic: the beautiful phrases he has rehearsed all the way home fail him as he enters his mother's house:

> S a kis szobába toppanék . . .
> Röpült felém anyám . . .
> S én csüggtem ajkán . . . szótlanúl . . .
> Mint a gyümölcs a fán.

And, as I stepped into the little room / My mother flew toward me; / and I hung on her lips wordlessly / Like the fruit on the tree. (87)

In "Egy estém otthon" ("One Evening at Home"), Petőfi described the newfound rapport with his father, who was still reluctant to accept the son's "profession," but now the poet could listen smilingly and accept his father's prejudices. Still, the poem makes it clear that the son was happy when his father enjoyed the drinking song he recited. The closeness of the family is apparent in all of these poems, yet this closeness is never described explicitly; it is intimated in the actions of the characters. Thus the mother's incessant questions about the poet's life are as much a sign of love as his father's grudging approval. Petőfi showed in the poem that he saw in each parent's characteristic behavior proofs of the love they have for him, and this love was amply returned. Similarly, the epistle, "István Öcsémhez" ("To My Younger Brother, István"), is concerned with the hardships his parents have had to endure and his desire to take some of the burdens off their shoulders. Though beginning in a seemingly light and frivolous tone, Petőfi soon changed to a serious mood and reminded his brother that their parents deserve all the care, love, and respect that they are able to give them.

Since the epistle is one of the genres Petőfi used successfully, and since this is an early yet far from immature example, it is informative to look at this poem in greater detail. The poem begins with the sort of general questions a letter home might contain:

Hát hogymint vagytok otthon, Pistikám?/
Gondoltok-e úgy néha-néha rám?
Mondjátok-e, ha estebéd után
Beszélgetéstek meghitt és vidám,
Mondjátok-e az est óráinál:
Hát a mi Sándorunk most mit csinál?
És máskülömben hogy van dolgotok?

And how are you at home, my little Pista? / Do you think of me now and then? / Do you remark, when after dinner / Your conversation is intimate and gay, / Do you say in the evening hours: / And what would our Sándor be doing now? / And generally, how are things with you? (109)

But soon it broaches the real subject:

Szegény atyánk! ha ő úgy nem bizik
Az emberekben: jégre nem viszik.
Mert ő becsületes lelkű, igaz;
Azt gondolá, hogy minden ember az.
És e hitének áldozatja lett,
Elveszte mindent, amit keresett.

Our poor father! Had he not trusted so / In men, they would not have ruined him. / Because he is honorable and true, He thought all men are the same. / And he became the victim of his trust: / Losing all that he had earned. (109)

In the closing lines, the poet expresses his regret at not being able to remove all burdens from his parents' shoulders and urges his brother to do what he can to help them. However, these lines take him too close to sentimentality, and so he concludes: "with these few lines, be satisfied, for now, my brother." The light tone he had sought escaped him and he felt he could no longer continue with the melancholy thoughts without becoming maudlin. The poem was written in 1844 after Petőfi's return to Pest following that first visit to his parents.

More often, when the problems were purely personal, Petőfi

turned to humor or satire. In "Egy telem Debrecenben" ("My Winter in Debrecen") he recounted the days of near starvation when often the only heat he had was the warmth of his pipe:

Pápista nem vagyok.
És mégis voltak böjtjeim, pedig nagyok.
Jó, hogy az embernek csontfoga van,
Ezt bölcsen rendelék az istenek,
Mert hogyha vas lett volna a fogam,
A rozsda ette volna meg. . . .

S az volt derék!
Ha verselék!
Ujjam megdermedt a hidegben,
És ekkor mire vetemedtem?
Hát mit tehettem egyebet?
Égő pipám
Szorítgatám,
Míg a fagy végre engedett.

I'm not a Papist / And still had fasts—but great ones. / It's good that one has teeth of bone— / The gods have decreed this wisely— / For if my teeth had been of iron, / Surely the rust would have eaten them. . . / Now that was something, / If I would compose! / My fingers were numb in the cold, / And so, what was I forced to do? / Well, what else could I do? / My burning pipe / I clutched / Until at last the freeze had thawed. (129–30)

Then, in a final defiant gesture, he concluded: "Ez ínségben csak az vigasztala, / Hogy ennél már nagyobb inségem is vala" ("In this misery all that consoled me / Was that I had been in even greater distress," 130).

Later, when his poetry was attacked for lack of decorum and refinement, for the use of unpoetic vocabulary and too real feelings and situations, he wrote a similarly flippant poem ("On My Bad Verses") stating that he intentionally wrote some bad poems to allow the critics something to chew on. After all, "if I am not mistaken, they too, are human," he remarked in these lines. The humorous Petőfi has often been ignored, yet he used comic devices both extensively and effectively. His satires, even when biting, are full of tongue-in-cheek humor. His epistles and lyrics contain a subtle, teasing humor. Many of his poems depend on a witty or jocose word or situation for effect. He exploited the humorous possibilities of rhyme and meter. Above all, he never ignored the cathartic possibilities of a broad smile or a hearty laugh.

III *Two Heroic Poems*

The early heroic poems, *A helység kalapácsa* (*The Hammer of the Village*) and *János Vitéz*, shared many of the qualities of the early lyrics. The humorous and satirical vein and the folk elements were important components of the poems. Petőfi experimented with language and style, although he did not depart drastically from the traditions and forms popular at the time. Thus, the narratives were reasonably successful, although the more "romantic" tale, *János Vitéz*, proved to be both more popular and more easily accepted by the critics.

A helység kalapácsa was the first of Petőfi's works to be published separately; it appeared a few weeks before the volume of his *Poems*. Written in mock-heroic style, it satirized the romantic epic tradition of the previous generations; however it also satirized society. This second line of attack, although witty and gentle, aroused the antagonism of some critics and readers. The poem was attacked for being unpoetic, uncouth, and generally unworthy of the genre. Many readers, and even some critics, missed the satire and were offended at what they assumed to be a realistically intended portrait of society.

The poem relates the story of the rivalry of the sexton Harangláb (Mr. Belfry) and the blacksmith, Fejenagy (Mr. Bighead) and the memorable battle between them engineered by the cowardly but clever clerk. The trivial incident is elaborated with epic trappings, yet even these devices remain true to the peasant atmosphere: the invocation uses words like "scary" (*rémítő*) and "to whoop" (*elkurjant*) to keep it from becoming too dignified. For example, Fejenagy uses this simile for his eagerness to see Erzsók: "Hozzád rohanok, / Mint a malacok gazdasszonaikhoz, / Ha kukoricát csörgetnek" ("Like pigs to the housewife / When corn is rattled, / I'll run to you," canto 3, p. 155).

Petőfi skillfully deflated the grand images of heroic poetry through such similes. He used a mixture of colloquialism and slang to support the parody. The result was a style that is a good reflection of the subject: the pretentiousness of many of the so-called heroic poems is made obvious and the reader can laugh at the incongruity of the epic devices, however distorted, used to describe naive villagers. Throughout, it is the narrator who assumes the epic pose; the characters behave, on the whole, unaffectedly and naturally. The nineteenth-century literary critic, Hugo Melzl, considered this parody as representing "nothing less than full emancipation from the Kisfaludi-Vörösmarty tradition of refined, but often stiff romanticism."[11] It was even more than that: It showed that Petőfi had rejected this style without ever using it more than appropriate for his purposes, and that he could use it at will.

Though Imre Vachot had urged Petőfi to write a mock-heroic poem, this one went beyond the satire he had expected. The break between the two men and Petőfi's eventual departure from their journal, the *Pesti Divatlap*, is explainable through the opposition of taste and temperament represented here: the serious, slightly stuffy gentlemen of the establishment could not accept the innovations of the young man. For, while the poem ridiculed linguistic and literary excesses, it also seemed to attack the ideals associated with the epic. Petőfi seemed intent on poking fun at stuffy village dignitaries and in so doing amuse his audience—and himself. The chapbook format of the first edition indicated that it was meant for the popular rather than the educated public. By showing the ridiculousness of grand poses in the case of the blacksmith, the innkeeper, and the others, he hoped to show the silliness of pretentiousness among his readers—the tradesmen and the professionals, and particularly their wives and daughters, who liked to imitate the fashions of the nobility.

The first canto introduces the hero, who, having gone to sleep during the Sunday evening service, finds himself locked in the church. He examines the options, and finally decides to let himself down by the bellpull—after he has had another nap. Meanwhile (canto 2), the rest of the village has gone to the tavern run by "the blushing Erzsók of the fifty-five year old charms." The mocking poet explains the origin of his heroine's epithet, twisting the epic manner to suit the tone of his poem:

Erzsók asszonyom ékes,
Holdkerek arculatán, . . .
Örökös hajnalnak
Pirja dereng,
S innen az elnevezés.
Vannak ugyan, kik
Állítni merészek,
Hogy Erzsók asszonyom arcát
Nem a szende szemérem,
Hanem a borital festette hasonlóvá
A hajnali pirhoz.
De ezek csak pletyka beszédek;
Mert Erzsók asszony nem is issza a bort . . .
Csak ugy önti magába.

On the adorned, moon-round visage / Of the good woman Erzsók / The rose of eternal dawn / breaks; / And from this the epithet. True, there are those, / Who dare affirm, / That the good woman Erzsók's face / Was not painted by bashful love / But rather by wine / To resemble the red of dawning. / But these are tales of gossips / For the good woman Erzsók does not drink wine— / She simply pours it into herself. (canto 2, pp. 140–41)

It is soon revealed that Erzsók has charmed not only the blacksmith, but the "tender-hearted" clerk also. Harangláb, the scheming sexton, had locked the blacksmith in the church to allow the clerk to reveal his love to Erzsók, which he proceeds to do now—after some encouragement from a pint of wine and Harangláb.

Fejenagy, having made his escape (canto 3) hurries to his Erzsók. When he enters the tavern, he sees the clerk on his knees before his lover, and, in a rage, starts to beat him; whereupon the "tender-hearted" man reveals the sexton's plot and the two enemies go to it in earnest, only prefacing the fight with some choice insults. The "lady" faints and soon the other men join the fray while the "peace-loving" shoemaker flees to summon the justice of the peace.

With some difficulty, Bagarja rouses the judge, who is taking his customary nap on the porch (canto 4), and relates the "great danger" that is threatening the village with extinction. He paints the battle in fittingly heroic terms:

Potyognak as emberek,
Mint a legyek őszi időben
A föld kifutott vértől
Olyan, mint a vörös posztó.

Men are falling, / Like flies in autumn. / The ground, from flowing blood / Is like red felt. (canto 4, p. 168)

Setting out, they stop for the judge's assistant and, as they pass the clerk's house, tell his wife the mischief he has been into. The "Amazon-natured Márta" promptly takes the lead to the tavern. Márta, true to her epithet, beats up her husband and drags him home. The judge puts a stop to the fight and claps the chief antagonist into the stocks. Fejenagy, however, consoles himself with the thought that he has defeated his enemy and upon his release will promptly propose to the "blushing Erzsók."

Petőfi concluded the poem with a "heroic epilogue," humorously claiming eternal fame for himself:

Azért én élni fogok,
Míg a világnak
Szappanbuboréka
Szét nem pattan.
Pislogni fog a hír mécse siromnak
Koszorús halmán,
Mint éjjel a macska szeme.

But yet I will live / As long as this soap bubble / Of the world / Does not burst. / The vigil light of fame will flicker / On the wreathed mound of my grave, / Like the cat's eye at night. (canto 4, p. 173)

It is hard to see how the first critics could have misread Petőfi's comic intentions. That they did shows the unsophisticated audiences the poets in the 1840s had to depend on. Poetry was supposed to be pretty and decorative; except for sentimental reasons, it was not supposed to engage the reader's emotions. Lyrics, especially if suitable for being set to music, were popular, but realistic scenes of rustic life were not. The poets of the Reform era had also found their audiences either unresponsive to their greatest works, or else pleased by the trappings of the narrative rather than by its theme, but since they broke no new ground in style, they were generally not attacked. Petőfi, an innovator, was often viciously censured. But, he remained true to his conviction that poetry should be a part of life, not an artificial world of overused images; he was also convinced that poetry should concern itself with the common people, the "folk," as well as the literate elements of the nation.

In this humorous poem, Petőfi portrayed village types without any effort to romanticize them. The blacksmith, somewhat lazy, is naturally bellicose and disdainful of those weaker than he. The mistress of the tavern is solid, hard-drinking, and generally able to keep order in her establishment, though on this occasion she does faint. The three Gypsies fit into the run-down tavern at the edge of the insignificant village: the cross-eyed violinist, the one-eyed cymbalist, and the lame player of the double bass make woeful music, yet are as much a part of the Sunday evening drinking and dancing as the ostler they follow into the tavern. The poet presented each character, each scene, briefly yet vividly. He extended the realistic detail to things like the justice's use of his old jacket as a pillow since the newer one had to be saved for such official functions as breaking up a fight.

On March 6, 1845, Petőfi's *János Vitéz* appeared. Unlike his first heroic poem, this one was immediately popular, and a second printing soon followed. To this financial success was added the critics' approval. The poem was praised for having captured the essence of the folk epic and the folktale. In many ways, the poem seemed to be little more than a versified folktale. It is only on closer examination that the several levels of meaning and the deeper concerns of the poet become apparent.

The poem remains a true folktale. The values, the aspirations, and the imaginative world of the Hungarian village influence its every aspect. The hero's actions, in particular, are ruled by the values of the village. The realism of the poem rests on this. Thus, instead of superimposing a mythology on his epic, Petőfi relied on the fantasy of the folktales. This was complemented by his portrayal of village types, so that all of the characters, whether the French king or the Turkish pasha, were recognizable as real persons. The hero, of course, remained an unaffected and unspoiled villager throughout—but not an unsophisticated one, nor one immune to temptations.

The success of the poem was due mainly to the skillful blending of the realistic and the fanciful. Petőfi was able to achieve this mixture in such a way that the realism did not deaden the fanciful and the imaginative parts did not carry the poem into unrealistic flights of fancy. The modern poet and critic Gyula Illyés attributed a "native soaring" to the poem, "which carries it in gradually rising circles, from the real Hungarian world to its heavenly copy, which is likewise 'Magyar.'"[12] The poem's success might be due to precisely this sense of a gradual ascent.

This movement, however, is hard to analyze. The poem is written in the "Hungarian alexandrine," or divided sixes. This had traditionally been a narrative meter, and the natural effect is strengthened by verses in which there are almost no departures from standard word order, and almost no archaic or unusual words. The poem, consequently, seems to be told by a folk narrator. Yet, through the seemingly simple style and natural language, the actual scene is merged with the psychological world of the protagonists. The opening lines show this clearly:

> Tüzesen süt le a nyári nap sugára
> Az ég tetejéről a juhászbojtárra.
> Fölösleges dolog sütnie oly nagyon,
> A juhásznak ugyis nagy melege vagyon.
>
> Szerelem tüze ég fiatal szivében,
> Ugy legelteti a nyájt a faluvégen.

The rays of the summer sun beat down / From the sky's zenith onto the shepherd lad, / But in vain do they burn so hot: The shepherd is quite warm already. / Love's fire glows in his youthful heart / As he feeds his flock at the edge of the village. (canto 1, p. 209)

The similes and metaphors of the poem reflect the method of the folksong and thus extend the richness of meaning found in each statement. The paralleling of external, natural objects with internal states enables the poet to make the reader aware of several levels of meaning in his poem. In the lovers' farewell, for example, the detailed description of the scene suits the characteristics of the two lovers whose every thought is of the other. At the same time, the protagonists think in terms of the phenomena that surround them. Thus, the reader becomes aware of the unity of man and nature through the seemingly simple statements of the lovers. János asks Iluska to remember him in these words: ". . . Ha látsz száraz kórót szélvésztöl kergetve, / Bujdosó szeretőd jusson majd eszedbe" (". . . If you see a dry stalk driven by the wind / Let your exiled lover come to your mind")—which are echoed by Iluska's answer: ". . . Ha látsz tört virágot útközépre vetve, / Hervadó szeretőd jusson majd eszedbe" ("If you see a broken flower flung on the highway / Let your fading lover come to your mind," canto 4, p. 216).

Through the poetry of such lines, a higher level of meaning is constantly suggested. The protagonists become cosmic figures rather than merely village lovers. Yet, on the literal level, nothing inappropriate for the two young villagers is said. Thus, gradually, the ascending order of the poem is established until the reincarnation in the final cantos becomes not only acceptable, but quite appropriate.

On the purely imaginative level, too, the blending of the psychical and physical is effective. A dry stalk driven aimlessly by the wind becomes a symbol of the aimless wandering of János, driven by grief. A faded flower appropriately symbolizes the grieving girl, deprived of the one person who had cared about her. Each image, further, suggests the fates that await the protagonists—death for Iluska and seemingly endless wanderings for János. Throughout the poem, Petőfi uses this device to change the common events into significant images. When, for example, János, or Jancsi as he is known familiarly, felt a great weight on his shoulders, he assumed that it is his heavy sheepskin cloak, but the poet reveals that it is really his heart that seemed to press so heavily on him.

Besides the sophisticated imagery and the subtle suggestion contained in such lines, Petőfi also used a more direct narrative device to achieve the upward movement. He set the scene in the village and ennobled both his hero and heroine and the values they represented. As in most tales, good and evil are sharply delineated, and the path to success is clearly marked. Opposed by evil (personified in their respective guardians), the lovers must show their faithfulness, perseverance, and bravery to be able to win happiness. These requirements apply particularly to the hero. Yet, both are guilty of negligence to their duties. This flaw sets the tale in motion, and Jancsi continues to act in accordance with the rules of the village. He is not expected to be perfect, but he does learn, as he faces progressively harder tasks, the ultimate of correct behavior. Furthermore, he never transgresses village mores in essential matters.

The concern with motivation, and particularly with the application of the classical rules that prescribe the sufferings of those who are slightly guilty rather than the wholly innocent, sets the poem apart from the fairy tale. So as not to depart too far from the atmosphere of the tale, Iluska remains an almost guiltless victim.

The poem opens with the idyllic afternoon the two lovers spend together, escaping for the moment the harsh realities of their lives. Unfortunately, Iluska's stepmother soon intrudes and drives the girl home while her lover frantically tries to collect his scattered sheep. Driven from his home on account of his negligence (he had merely been tolerated as a hired hand by his now-dead foster mother's husband), Jancsi sets out to try his fortune in the world after a tearful and tender farewell from his Iluska. What he most regrets is that there will be no one to protect her now (cantos 1–4).

The fifth canto is a miniature idyll of the *puszta* (steppe), although Jancsi remains in the center of it: he is still walking on the endless plains when the sun rises to show a barren scene. Though the sun brightens everything on the horizon, "Jancsi trudges on with his dark shadow / And the dark thoughts in his mind." At noon he stops by a pond to eat, drink, and sleep, only to be awakened by a sudden storm whose thunder breaks into his dreams just as he is about to kiss Iluska.

The realistic touches—János eating the last of his bacon, using the brim of his felt hat for a cup, and a mole's mound for a pillow, his turning the sheepskin cloak inside out to ward off the rain—reaffirm the hero's basic humanity and his will to live. These touches also emphasize the matter-of-fact acceptance of all that he meets and the natural impulse to make the best of things. Though he has no set goals, he is not a despairing, resigned, world-weary hero either. In Jancsi there is nothing of the romantic traveler seeking to lose himself in the wilds of the Harz mountains or among the beauties of the Rhine. Instead of the passivity of the romantic heroes there is a determination to be active in a constructive and basically moral way. He is always on the side of good.

The first night János reaches a seemingly deserted inn only to find that it is a robbers' hideout. These are real criminals, not the runaway peasant boys or political "exiles" who figure as *betyárok* ("outlaws") in Hungarian literature, but *zsiványok* ("bandits"): real evildoers for whom robbery and murder are a way of life. Pretending to join them, Jancsi tricks the group and burns the inn over them as they lie in a drunken stupor. The importance of this conclusion to the first movement is that the hero refuses to take the plunder. Though tempted by the seemingly easy way out of his and his sweetheart's dilemma, he rejects the temptation:

"Hozzájok sem nyúlok . . . azt én nem tehetem,
Nincs elromolva a lelkiismeretem.—
Édes szép Iluskám, csak viseld terhedet,
Bízd a jóistenre árva életedet!"

"I'll not even touch these; that I cannot do; / My conscience is not ruined. / My dear Iluska, you must bear your burdens, / And trust to God your orphan life." (canto 4, p. 222)

In these few lines, Petőfi established the hero's moral greatness, but did this without moralizing. Also, he was able to lead his hero to the realization of the goal he must have: to win wealth honestly and thus return to Iluska. By the end of the first section (cantos 1–6) the poet had established the conditions under which Jancsi was to continue his journey.[13]

In this section and the next one Petőfi also showed that the values that were to prevail in the poem were those of the village. Just as taking the robbers' gold would have been condemned by the village, Jancsi's return from his adventures with wealth would have seemed inappropriate: most soldiers had stories to tell of great opportunities missed; none came back with great wealth. Thus, the second section (cantos 7–18) must end inconclusively. Seemingly, it ends in tragedy, for a simple happy ending would not be realistic. The lovers are to be reunited, but only after Jancsi has overcome the evils that caused their separation, namely, the tyranny of his master and of Iluska's stepmother. This, however, has to be achieved on a symbolic level, and only comes after the hero has gone through the initiation of a series of successful adventures.

Having rejected the robber's gold, Jancsi sets out to make good in the traditional way of the peasant boys: he joins the hussars, sees many lands, and has many adventures. In Tataria, the Saracen king turns out to be their friend; in Taljania (Italy) János and his companions brave the snowy mountains and so reach Poland. They then travel to India and so reach France to aid the king against the Turks. In these cantos (cantos 7–10) fabulous, but not magical, elements are introduced. The basic realism is retained, because all that happens is based on the tales of veterans returning from service in the Habsburg armies. The historical and geographical facts are condensed and shaped by the narrator: Tatars and Turks are enemies, the Poles and the French are friends, and the Italian Alps are higher than any mountains a Lowlander would see. Only the English critic of the *Athenaeum* could have found difficulty in the geographic inconsistencies in the poem, not realizing that this is the same sort of "freedom" Shakespeare exercised in endowing Bohemia with a seacoast.

The adventure in France earns János the epithet "vitéz" (i.e., hero or knight), when he kills the Turkish leader and rescues the French princess. It also brings him to the second and more difficult temptation: the princess wants to marry him, and he must refuse if he is to remain true to his Iluska. The realistic undertone of the poem is also reestablished in these scenes. Jancsi remains quite natural and unaffected. He answers the princess' proposal by suggesting they speak to her father first—as would be proper in his village. The words he uses are in the realm of the village also: "Menjünk rózsám, elébb az édesatyádhoz. /Ott majd közelebbről vizsgáljuk a dolgot" ("Let us go, my rose, first to your father, / Then we can consider the matter more closely," canto 12, p. 232). Returning to the court, the hussars are given a grand feast. They do justice to the food and the wines, but eventually the king interrupts to request the hero of the day to relate his story.

Explaining his surname, Kukoricza (Corn), János tells the king that he was found by a rich farmer's wife in the cornfield and was raised by her. In time, he came to know the other orphan of the village, and fell in love with her. Then, one day, he was driven from the village, and so set out on his adventures. János thus uses the story to give the princess a polite refusal. The king gives him a fortune in gold and jewels to enable him to marry his sweetheart, but the homeward journey proves disastrous: a storm wrecks his ship and he can only escape by forcing a griffin to carry him home. The supernatural is thus brought into the story, but only briefly. Alighting at the edge of the village, János reenters the real world. Petőfi deftly sketched the activity of the village, but focused on the human emotions:

> "Nem hozok aranyat, nem hozok kincseket,
> De meghozom régi hűséges szívemet,
> És ez elég neked, drága szép Iluskám!
> Tudom, hogy nehezen vársz te is már reám."
>
> Ily gondolatokkal ért a faluvégre,
> Érintette fülét kocsiknak zörgése,
> Kocsiknak zörgése, hordóknak kongása;
> Szüretre készült a falu lakossága.
>
> Nem figyelmezett ő szüretre menőkre,
> Azok sem ismertek a megérkezőre;
> A falu hosszában ekképen haladott
> A ház felé, ahol Iluskája lakott.

"I bring no gold, no treasures, / But I do bring my faithful heart; / This will content you, my precious Iluska. / I know you, too, await me eagerly." / Thinking such thoughts he reached the village edge / Where the rattle of wagons struck his ears; / The rattle of wagons, the rumbling of barrels: / The village was readying for the wine harvest. / He did not note the harvesters / Nor did they recognize the new arrival: / Through the length of the village he went / To the house where his Iluska had lived." (canto 17, p. 242)

Learning that she had died in his absence, he plucks a rose from her grave and sets out again, taking this memento as his sole companion.

The final part of the poem (cantos 19–27) begins with his new adventures and leads to the hero's triumphs. Though these are in some ways parallel to the earlier adventures, János has moved beyond the realistic world. Still, Petőfi is careful of the transitions: János' first adventure is to help a pedlar whose wagon is stuck in the mud. With this good deed behind him, he strolls into the deep forest. Here, the magic world begins: the hero defeats the sentry of the land of the giants, and reaches their castle. Using his wits and strength, he kills the king, whereupon the terrified sons pledge their loyalty.

Drawn by an undefined need, however, he continues his journey. The format of the fairy tale and the folktale demands this, and the same conventions also demand that he exterminate the witches both as representatives of evil and as the agents of his personal tragedy. With the help of the giants even the last one, Iluska's stepmother, is killed. As a result, evil is destroyed:

> Sötétség országa kiderült végképpen,
> Örökös homálynak napfény lett helyében,
> János vitéz pedig rakatott nagy tüzet,
> A tűz minden seprőt hamuvá égetett.

The land of darkness lit up forever; / Instead of eternal twilight, sunlight ruled; / And János Vitéz had a huge bonfire made / To burn each and every broom to ashes. (canto 20, p. 253)

Though his sorrow is no longer intense, János still remembers his Iluska. As a premonition of what is to follow, he unknowingly spends a night in a cemetery. The ghosts prepare to carry him off, but then the cock crows and all supernatural beings disperse. The hero, after all, must find his own way to his Iluska. This canto also serves to reestablish the realistic mood—all things are seen more clearly in the morning—and to lead into the last and final adventure. The last stanza of this section is particularly effective. As the crowing of the rooster awakens János, he shivers because a cold wind is blowing, and rises to resume his wanderings. His path now leads to a mountaintop at the edge of a marvelously tranquil sea.

This sea is the Operenciás ocean, that is, the sea which surrounds the world, and where the world ends. János once again summons a giant to aid him across this sea. Sighting an island in the middle, they head for that instead: it is Fairyland. But, before he can enter, János must overcome three obstacles. Defeating the three bears, the three lions, and the three-headed dragon, the hero finally reaches the land of eternal spring, only to be overcome by despair: how could he be happy here where everyone is happy, without his beloved? Determined to end his life in the lake, he throws in the rose he had plucked from Iluska's grave and wades in after it. Suddenly, the maiden herself rises from the waves. This is the Water of Life; the rose, which had captured her essence, is restored into her. Enraptured by the beauty of the pair, the fairies joyfully crown them king and queen.

This, briefly, is the story. The charm and richness of the poem, however, is dependent on the masterful blending of realism and fantasy in a genre that is by definition unrealistic. Its first successes were due to these qualities. The allegorical meaning was often ignored, yet any analysis of the poem must return to the basic realism. This is constantly present in both the incidents and the language. When the stepmother comes upon Jancsi and Iluska making love, her abuse fits what would be expected of a village crone. Similarly, it is the moral values of the village that force Jancsi to leave, since it would not be proper to argue with the man who has stood in his father's place. Refusing to join the robbers is also the only real alternative János has: if he becomes a criminal, he can never return to the village to claim his Iluska.

Of course, not everything is accepted as the absolute truth: there is a suspension of disbelief, as well as an occasional exaggeration that is accepted as such. But this does not lessen the basic reality. The characters in the tale are figures familiar to the audience: the cook, with the meal ready, just as a good housewife would have it; the king who sounds like a well-to-do and kindly farmer when he says, "Just go on and speak, my son, we'll be sure to listen," or

> ". . . Tartóztatnálak, de tudom, nem maradnál,
> Kivánkozol lenni máris galambodnál,

Eredj tehát–hanem társid maradjanak;
Éljenek itt néhány mulatságos napnak."

I'd have told you to stay, but I know you'd not listen, / You're already wishing to be with your dove; / Go then–but let your comrades stay; / Let them remain here for a few merry days. (canto 16, p. 238)

Through these touches, Petőfi insured that the setting and characterization remained true to the folktale.

Similarly, in describing the battle, Petőfi avoided the flowery speeches and threats of epic heroes and gave the central scenes in idiomatic, rustic words:

Hej csinálom-adta! meleg egy nap volt ez,
Hegyé emelkedett már a török holttest.
De a basa még él mennykő nagy hasával,
S Kukoricza Jancsit célozza vasával.

Hey! what a hot day this was, / The Turkish bodies already rose mountain-high, / But the big-bellied pasha still lives / And aims his steel at Kukoricza Jancsi. (canto 12, p. 230)

At other times, the lyricism of which the poet has such command helps establish the realism:

Hanem János vitéz nem figyelt e szóra,
Feje fölött repült egy nagy sereg gólya;
Őszre járt az idő: ezek a madarak
Bizonyosan szülőföldéről szálltanak.

Szelíd epedéssel tekintett utánok,
Mintha azok neki jó hírt mondanának,
Jó hírt Iluskáról, szép Iluskájáról,
S oly régen nem látott kedves hazájáról.

But János Vitéz did not hear these words, / For above his head flew a flock of storks: / Autumn was approaching and these birds / Most likely came from the land of his birth. / With gentle longing he watched them / As if they were giving him good news, / Good news from Iluska, his beautiful Iluska, / And from his so long unseen dear homeland. (canto 16, pp. 239–40)

Finally, the hero's fidelity to his Iluska, who is constantly on his mind, and even the loss of the treasure given him by the king, are elements in establishing the realism of the poem. No proper hero would forget his lover, no matter what the temptation, and no bragging soldier ever returned to his village with the fabulous fortune he had won, but lost it all through some fantastic adventure.

Even in the third and superficially most fantastic part, the basic realism remains. The tale must have a happy ending, but it would not be believable for the lovers to be reunited and "live happily ever after" in their own village. Thus, to "reconcile realism and poetic justice," János' way must lead to "the world where the rules of realism are no longer valid,"[14] namely, the world of the fairy tale. Here, the hero overcomes all obstacles. Thus, the third part becomes the final act in the realization of his dream. This is not accomplished without the aid of supernatural creatures (giants, fairies). Yet in the tradition of such tales, these creatures are in some way dependent on the hero. Furthermore, János remains a wanderer: he has no peace of mind until his sweetheart is restored to him. The miracle of the Water of Life accomplishes this, and the hero can end his search.

The surface glitter charmed the first readers, and the realistic structure has entertained later audiences. Beyond these attractions, the "epic" quality has often been attributed to this poem. While neither its length nor its structure justify that appellation, it has become known as a "folk epic." Perhaps a better term would be "heroic folk poem": it glorifies the values and the heroes of the village, i.e., of the people. As a record of a resourceful and brave young man's struggle against seemingly impossible odds, told without sentimentality, it also has a heroic quality. D. Mervyn Jones found the best explanation for the poem's popularity in the words of F. L. Lucas on Homer's *Odyssey*: it is "not merely a tale of changes and chances in perilous seas, it is a tale of loyalties that all those changes and chances failed, in the end, to break."[15]

CHAPTER 3

New Themes, New Styles

I *Turbulent Months*

IN 1845–1846, for a period of about eighteen months, Petőfi went through a personal crisis which is reflected in his poetry, and which seems to have resulted in the development of a new and stronger style. He experimented with a variety of devices, styles, and poses, as well as a range of vocabulary and images that allowed him to explore the poetic heritage of the storm and stress and romanticism to a degree his earlier poems had not done. The emphasis on the inner world—the poet's emotions, desires, and wishes—prepared him to write the highly emotional yet fully controlled lyrics of the next period. It is almost as if one could see, in the development of this one young poet, the maturing of the romantic movement from the undirected and unrestrained emotionalism of its precursors to the distilled perfection of a Keats or a Shelley where emotion, though intense, is never out of control, and where poetic imagery and evocative language is always subordinated to the meaning and purpose of the poem.

Furthermore, this period shows a change in subjects, particularly the nonpersonal ones, from the traditional school of regrets to the beginnings of a positive program of political and social reform. By the summer of 1846 a poet sure of his style, confirmed in the rightness of his choice of profession and vocation, and in command of a new and definitely personal style, emerged. The series of personal triumphs which followed, though not free of setbacks, were an extra bonus, but were not responsible for the change in Petőfi's style. That was a result of months of hard thinking and experimentation.

In 1845–1846, two cycles of love poetry, each commemorating an unfortunate love affair, appeared. The first, *Cipruslombok*

Etelke Sírjáról (*Cypress Leaves from the Tomb of Etelke*), written after the death of Etelke Csapó, the fifteen-year-old sister-in-law of Sandór Vachott, was a memorial to an ideal. Petőfi was more in love with the romantic trappings of longing and unfulfilled love than with the young girl. The influence of Novalis and Young is obvious, yet the emotion was sincere enough: he mourned himself, even if not the girl. In the early poems the preoccupation with the beauty of the dead girl and the details of the burial were morbid, though suited to the expectations of the readers. The poet mourned the loss of the happy love he had anticipated. "Ha ébren meg nem látogatsz" ("If you do not visit me when awake") discharged the obligatory affirmation that even a ghostly bride would be better than none. In "Én vagyok itt" ("It is I here") he commemorated one of the many nights spent in the cemetery by her grave. But, when he escaped the maudlin sentiments that characterized most of the thirty-four poems and approached the folksong in tone and imagery, he could be successful. This is seen in "Te voltal egyetlen virágom" ("You were my only flower"). In the economical style that marks his best poetry, he set up the meaningful parallels that had been destroyed by her death:

Te voltal egyetlen virágom;
Hervadt vagy: puszta életem.
Te voltál fényes napvilágom;
Lementél: éj van körülem.

Te voltál képzeményim szárnya:
Megtörve vagy: nem szállhatok.
Te voltál vérem forrósága;
Meghűltél: oh majd megfagyok.

You were my only flower: / Now you are withered, my life is a wasteland. / You were my bright sunlight: / Now you have set: night surrounds me. / You were the wings of my fantasy; / Now you are broken: I cannot fly. / You were the seething of my blood; / Now you are cold: oh! I am freezing. (288)

The last few poems reported his acceptance of her death. "Time is a mighty physician," he wrote, and looked forward to happier times. Finally, in "Messze vándoroltam" ("I have wandered far") sorrow and mourning crystallized into a lyrical experience. Though the poem began with a series of macabre images, it concluded on a peaceful note. The poet reached this calm through a logical analysis of what he would like to have done and what it was possible for him to do:

> . . . Nyugodt már kebelem. Fájdalmam szélvésze
> Kitombolt, elzúgott, megszűnt, elenyésze.
>
> Alvó tenger a mult. Halálod a kőszirt,
> Amelyen reményim sajkája kettétört,
> Ez a durva kőszirt most már olyan szépen
> Áll a látkör végén a kék messzeségben; . . .

My breast is at peace. / The whirlwind of my sorrow / Has spent its fury, is past, over, dead. / The past is a sleeping sea; your death, / The cliff on which the vessel of my hopes was dashed! / These rough rocks now stand so beautifully / At the edge of the horizon in the blue distance. (331)

Petőfi, an intensely emotional and personal poet, seemed to have used this experience to move from his earlier lyrical style, based mostly on the objective persona of the folksong, to a more subjective exploitation of the poetic styles he was developing. The depersonalized quality of the completed cycle is further evidenced by its publication in March, barely three months after Etelka's death. Significantly, Petőfi donated the profit from fifty copies (about fifteen hundred *pengős*) to the people of Árva and Szepes counties who were faced with famine.[1]

Szerelem gyöngyei (*The Pearls of Love*), the second cycle of love poems (1845), recorded Petőfi's feelings for Berta Mednyánszky. Meeting this rich and attractive girl six months after the death of Etelka, Petőfi chose her to fill the gap in his life. Again, the poems speak more of the poet's feelings than of the girl: he was in love with love and when Berta rejected his proposal, he did not waste much time regretting it. Here, as in the *Cipruslombok*, Petőfi was developing an individualized and subjective lyrical style to supplant his earlier poses. The "I" of these poems was no longer a village lad or a *betyár*. He was also perfecting the richness of his imagery through these poems in which the passionate content was clothed in musing tones:

Oly szelíd, szép őszi délután van!
Itt-ott látni csak kis felleget;
A viharból ugy maradt meg ez, mint
Bús időkből az emlékezet.

Such a gentle, quiet autumn afternoon! / Only here and there a little cloud, / Left over from the storm / Like a memory of sorrowful times. ("Elnemult a fergeteg"; "The Storm has Subsided," 366)

In another poem, the images were concentrated to express the intensity of his desire:

Fa leszek, ha fának vagy virága.
Ha harmat vagy; én virág leszek.
Harmat leszek, ha te napsugár vagy . . .
Csakhogy lényink egyesüljenek.

I'll be a tree, if you are its blossom; / If you are the dew, a flower I'll become. / I'll be the dew, if you are a sunbeam, / That our two being may unite in one. ("Fa leszek ha"; "I'll Be a Tree, if," 362)

These love poems represent only a small portion of Petőfi's output at this time. As always, he was writing a great deal on a variety of themes, though most of the works of this period were experimental. Early in 1845 he made a tour of the northern counties and sent back a prose report under the title, "Úti jegyzetek" ("Travel notes") to the capital. In these, he commented on the poverty, ignorance, and the loss of Magyar identity he often observed among the common people of the region, but the overall tone of the letters was objective and frequently humorous. He ridiculed the reactionary manners and empty political activity of the petty nobility, but there was little bitterness. Also notable, and an innovation in the travelogue, was the lack of didacticism. Petőfi presented the scene and the people pretty much as he saw them. The roads were wretched and the inns bad, but he described the scenes with a poetic touch. An occasional historical digression or an anecdote varied the pace. These letters are interesting chiefly for the insight they give into Petőfi's personality, but they also capture many of the qualities that were to make his genre pictures and landscape poems successful.

These letters were all the more interesting because, in 1845,

Petőfi seemed dissatisfied with both his personal achievements and the political situation. In fact, he was affected by a deep depression by the latter half of the year, from which he did not emerge until late 1846. Many of his writings at this time exhibited a depressingly dark side of Hungarian society, and of mankind in general. Much of his work was artistically inferior to the bulk of his poetry, of interest chiefly for the information these give on the development of the poet's style and of his personality. "Zöld Marci," a drama about a highwayman, was rejected by the theaters and subsequently destroyed by the author. Judging from *Tigris és hiéna* (*The Tiger and the Hyena*), a historical drama written in 1846, it must have been a late romantic offshoot of *Die Räuber* by Schiller. A novella written in these months of depression, *A hóhér kötele* (*The Hangman's Rope*) and a verse romance, *Salgó*, are both characterized by a hothouse atmosphere of revenge and hatred. Though the latter, like *Tigris és hiéna*, has a historical setting, and the former is contemporary, gothic horrors are not spared in either. The theme of thwarted and betrayed love, followed by revenge, is also seen in "Szilaj Pista," a shorter and in some ways better verse tale.

In general, his poetry at this time seems unaffected by the books he was then reading. The meditative lyrics of Csokonai, the revolutionary poems of Béranger, and the world-weary irony of Heine were to be found in a haphazard collection with heroes modeled on Shakespeare's passionate figures and clothed in Hungarian costumes. Byron and Shelley also exerted their influence, and as yet Shelley's idealism had not replaced the Byronic hatred of the world too often evident in these transitional works. Some poems, moreover, were dominated by "romantic" excesses: *Salgó* not only has a medieval setting, it introduces robber barons, kidnapping of the enemy's daughter, rivalry of the father and son for her love, and cold-blooded revenge which ends in the extermination of the entire family as well as the heroine's death. Still, as the critic János Horváth pointed out, this period of intense and sometimes confusing activity was necessary both to provide an objective correlative for Petőfi's own overwrought emotions and to enable him to find his own voice. The style of the naive lyric was no longer sufficient for what he had to say, but he had found no new form. It was through this period of experimentation that the "mature poetic personality" of Petőfi was to emerge.[2]

Balance was also lacking in Petőfi's personal life. He often identified with his tormented heroes, so that the impersonality needed in true art was absent. This, again, is traceable to his troubled personal situation. Financially, he was in perilous circumstances. His relationship with Vachot became more and more strained as the editor tried to reduce Petőfi's contribution to their joint venture. Critics attacked his works, or, even worse, were silent. His friends seemed to have deserted him, and his parents' hand-to-mouth existence was a source of constant worry. In 1846 he helped form the Society of Ten (Tízek Társasága),[3] a writer's "guild" determined to force publishers to deal more fairly with the contributors to their publications. The strike they initiated failed, but not without Petőfi's challenging Vachot to a duel for copyright infringements. The practical publisher refused to meet him, and, lacking legal safeguards, Petőfi had to give up the strike and be content with a moral victory.

Thus, much of the poetry of this time, including the sixty-six lyrics of the *Felhők* (*Clouds*, 1846) cycle was composed in a melancholy, world-weary mood. Nevertheless, most of them were experiments in a stronger language and new, effective lyrical forms. Petőfi commented on friends who had deserted him ("To Faithless Friends") and on the malicious attacks of the critics ("Base World"; "Out, to the Open Air"; "To His Lordship, Ferenc Csaszár")· But, in the best poems, he went beyond personal suffering to lash out not so much against enemies as at the injustice he saw around him. "As őrűlt" ("The Madman"), a dramatic monologue reminiscent of *King Lear*, is such a work. It opens with an account of the speaker's imagined death by poisoning and progresses to cursing the hypocrisy and artificiality of the world. The hypocrisy of the killers is given proper treatment, yet what captures the imagination is the crazy man's vow of revenge. Buried in Africa, he offers his heart to the hyena who is poisoned by it:

. . . De hiába, csak így jár,
Ki emberrel tesz jót. Mi az ember?
Mondják: virágnak gyökere,

Amely fönn a mennyben virúl.
De ez nem igaz.
Virág az ember, melynek gyökere
Ott lenn van a pokolban.

But then, this is how one fares / If he benefits mankind. What is man? / They say: the root of the flower / Which blossoms up in heaven. / But this is not true. / He is the flower whose root / Is down in hell. (431)

Nothing good happens in this evil world, and even God's tears turn to mud: A soldier's reward is a ragged uniform, all women are fickle and love, though one drop of it is "sweeter / Than a sea turned to honey," is also more lethal "Than a sea turned to poison." Finally, the world is a rotten fruit and unless the last judgment comes on the morrow, he will blow it up.

The poem, written in free verse, uses the speaker's laughter ("Ha, ha, ha!") as a sort of refrain. It starts *in medias res* with the crazy man commanding all to leave him alone to allow him to finish his great work: he will make a whip of flames from the sun's rays to scourge the world. The poem thus reflects the wandering of a disturbed mind around a fixed idea and in a sense captures Petőfi's disturbed poetic vision in a realistic and objective manner. The effect was cathartic, for in the following months a lighter tone gradually entered Petőfi's poetry even though the depression was not immediately lifted: the poet's situation and expectations also had to change.

Concerned as he seemed with personal grievances, Petőfi was not solely preoccupied with them. More and more of his poems were political in tone or intent. In a satiric portrait of the Hungarian nobleman ("A magyar nemes") he touched on a theme of the "Úti jegyzetek": the members of this class—once justly glorified for its defense of the country—now allowed their swords to rust and spent lazy days living off the work of the peasants, smoking their pipes, eating, and drinking. The poem used a truncated line and *a a b b* rhyme, with the fourth line, "I am a Hungarian nobleman," as the refrain. The quick tempo and proud refrain underscored the irony, as did the general construction of each stanza. The speaker revealed himself by reference to his preoccupations:

Tán a tudománynak éljek?
A tudósok mind szegények.
Nem írok, nem olvasok.
Én magyar nemes vagyok! . . .

Mit törődom a hazával?
A hazának száz bajával?
Majd elmulnak a bajok.
Én magyar nemes vagyok!

Should I live for knowledge? / Scholars are all poor. / I neither read nor write. / I'm a Hungarian nobleman . / . . . / What care I about the country? / And its hundred problems, / The problems will go away, / I'm a Hungarian nobleman. (400)

Other poems were also concerned with the decline of Hungary as a nation, which the poet attributed to this decline of patriotism. One of the more elegiac of these poems is "A hazáról" ("About the Homeland") in which the quiet, resigned tone is enhanced by the form: the last two lines of each quatrain become progressively longer (eight, then nine and ten syllables) although the three stresses remain constant. This progressively slower cadence is further strengthened by a strong midline caesura and a combination of letter sounds that force even more internal stops—very few of the words can be elided, and often a full stop is required. The effect is that of a melancholy walk; one could not even call it a funeral march. Furthermore, the somber mood evoked by the metrics is echoed in the imagery:

Lement a nap. De csilagok
Nem jöttenek. Sötét az ég.
Közel s távolban semmi fény nincs,
Csak mécsvilágom s honszerelmem ég.

Szép csillag a honszeretet,
Gyönyörüségesen ragyog.
Szegény hazám, szegény hazám te,
Neked kevés van ilyen csillagod.

Mécsemnek lángja mint lobog!
Mitől lobog? mi lengeti?

Éjfélt ütött. Ti lengtek itten
Mécsem körül, ti népem ősei!

The sun has set. But the stars / Have not come. The sky is dark. / There is no light near or far; / Only my vigil light and my patriotism burns. / A beautiful star is the love of fatherland, / And brightly it shines. / My poor homeland, my poor homeland, You / Have few such stars. / My candle's light—how it flames! / Why did it flare up? What has stirred it so? / It has struck midnight. You drift here, you / Ancestors of my race! (414)

The poem goes on to recall the glorious past when the Magyars conquered Europe and when the Hungarian domains reached to the seas in the south, north, and east. Finally, it asks whether Hungarian glory was merely a falling star, or a comet that came and went, only to return in later centuries. Thus, the poet returned to the original images, having ranged from stars to candles to the suggestion of a beacon in the night.

In "Isten csodája" ("God's miracle") Petőfi struck a more determined tone and asserted that only a miracle had kept the nation intact under numerous disasters: internal strife, Tatar and Turkish invasions, foreign rule. He then urged the nation to look to the remedies itself, rather than always trust to good fortune to survive. This more militant tone was to become characteristic of Petőfi. With it, he turned away from the traditional patriotic poetry of Vörösmarty and Kölcsey and their school, which had concentrated on past glories and did not present a program for the future. The program, even with Petőfi, was not yet formed. The positive tone, however, emerged ever more strongly in his writing, until he became the poet of the Independence movement calling for future deeds as great as those of the past, and indeed, praising the soldiers of the Revolution as worthy descendants of their brave ancestors.

Finally, in one of his best descriptive-narrative poems,[4] Petőfi took a common landmark of the arid, deserted lowlands, the ruins of a *csárda* (country inn), and made it a metaphor for the decline of the country. The poem opens as a paean to these plains, the poet's favorite landscape for they remind him of freedom: "Puszta, puszta, te vagy a szabadság képe, / És szabadság, te vagy lelkem istensége!" ("*Puszta, puszta*, you are the image of freedom, / And Freedom, you are the god of my soul," 402). As he offers his life for freedom in subsequent verses, the poet is almost sentimental, but he quickly returns to reality: "De mi ez? sir . . . halál . . . hova nem vetődtem! / Nem csoda külömben, mert rom van elöttem." ("But what is this? . . . the grave . . . death . . . where have I gotten to! /But no wonder, since a ruin stands before me," 403). Journeying through the prairie, he comes upon the ruins of the *csárda*. Since a stone ruin is a rarity here, he seeks an explanation. This is briefly given: a village or city once stood here, but the Turks have destroyed it and left only a half-ruined church. A parenthetical expression brings the poem back to the idea of lost liberty: "Poor Hungary, my poor homeland, / How many different chains you have already worn!" The narrative is then resumed.

In time, then, an inn was built from the church, but those who once lodged there are now long dead. The inn has lost its roof, its door and its window are indistinguishable, and all that remains is the sweep of the well on top of which a lone eagle sits, meditating on mutability. In the final four lines the scene changes and a more optimistic note is struck:

Fölötte lángol a nap, az égnek ifja,
Lángol, mert kebelét a szerelem vívja;
Szeretője, aki epedve néz rája,
Délibáb, a puszták szép tündérleánya.

Above him blazes the sun, the sky's youthful son, / He blazes, for his heart is full of love; / His lover, who longingly watches him, / Is the *délibáb*,[5] the beautiful fairy maid of the *pusztas*. (404)

The parallel between the decline of the nation and the slow ruin of the church-inn is established, but, as in the best of Petőfi's allegory, not belabored. In fact, the lone eagle, though slightly suggestive of the Habsburgs, is as forlorn as the rest of the scene, and by the closing lines Petőfi's concentration on the scene beyond these ruins suggests a renewal.

In this poem, Petőfi again turned to the subjects and themes that allowed him to speak of his own feelings through external objects, and when he did this, his poetry remained lucid and calm without losing the intensity of the passionate personal lyric.

The inner world received emphasis. The poet confessed his desolation, but also revealed himself as the sun in love with a beautiful and unreachable ideal.

Poems such as this (and there are a score or more altogether) showed the effects of Petőfi's experimentation with a new form even before the break with the traditional forms was complete. Most of them reflect Petőfi's "true lyrical voice: dreamy, gentle, pensive . . . an almost motionless state of the soul."[6] The themes range from love to life's goals, to a desire for glory, to a recurring wish for death in the cause of his country and Liberty. These last two were soon to become one and the same for Petőfi.

II *Between the Old and the New*

Petőfi used the counterpointing of his feelings by reference to the objective world successfully in "A négy-ökrös szekér" ("The Ox Cart"). The poem recounts a hayride and seems at first to be nothing more than a diary entry, although the images in the second stanza lend it a delightful quality that suggests an evening removed from time and place, floating in an enchanted sphere:

Világos éj volt. A hold fenn vala;
Halványan járt a megszakadt felhőkben,
Miként a bús hölgy, aki férjinek
Sírhalmát keresi a temetőben.
Kalmár szellő járt a szomszéd mezőkön,
S vett a füvektől édes illatot.
Az országúton végig a szekérrel
A négy ökör lassacskán ballagott.

It was a bright evening. The moon was high; / She walked faintly among the broken clouds / Like the sorrowing wife seeking / Her husband's grave in the churchyard. / The merchant breeze moved over the neighboring leas / And bought sweet scents from the grasses. / Down the highway, pulling the cart / The four oxen plodded slowly. (395)

The gently grieving mood and the sweet-scented breeze is full of magical suggestiveness, but the plodding reality of the four oxen anchors the scene in this world. Thus, the magic of the everyday is suggested. Then, turning to his companion, the speaker gives the poem a more serious, even a somber turn:

> "Ne válasszunk magunknak csillagot?"
> Szólék én ábrándozva Erzsikéhez,
> "A csillag vissza fog vezetni majd
> A mult időknek boldog emlékéhez,
> Ha elszakaszt a sors egymástul minket."
> S választottunk magunknak csillagot.
> Az országúton, etc.

"Should we not chose ourselves a star?" / I said dreamily to Erzsike, / "The star will lead us back / To the happy memories of former times / If fate should separate us from each other." / And we chose ourselves a star. / Down the highway, etc. (395)

Such mingling of magic and reality, of a serene, peaceful, and even happy setting and the premonition of tragedy, was often found in Petőfi's poetry, and particularly in the meditative poems, almost as if he felt that his life would be brief and that there would be few happy moments. But, he was not morbid or depressing: only in a few poems did despair dominate, and even there, the melancholy was tempered. Though he indulged in some moments of self-pity or in sentimental mourning over his and the world's miseries, Petőfi almost always moved away from this through the imagery of the poems or the expressed determination to make the best of things.

"Tündérálom" ("Fairy Dream") stands at the end of this period of Petőfi's poetry. Though rooted in reality (either a chance meeting with his childhood playmate or a brief yet intense passion in the summer of 1839), it is not so much a love poem as a lyrical-psychological confession. Written in iambic pentameters, the eight-line stanzas are rhymed *a b c b b d b d*, so that the *b* rhyme subtly connects the two halves. Its real theme, in spite of the poet's explicit statement that he has here conjured up "first love," is the search for happiness. As such, the poem fits the preoccupations of 1845–1846. Furthermore, many of the trappings of romanticism are found here also: we are reminded of Novalis and his search for the Blue Flower; the longing for the heavenly or the divine; the description of personified Ideas. But here all these elements are blended into a new poem: it is almost impossible to trace a specific influence, and all that can be said is that the poem expresses some of the best of the idealized poetry of the romantic movement without ever quite losing touch with reality. Petőfi had by now developed the new style with which he had been experimenting and gained the mastery that he had lacked in the two cycles of love poetry and in *Felhők*.

The poem owes its success partly to the images through which the everyday world is constantly brought in contact with the ethereal without disturbing it in the slightest:

> Sajkás vagyok vad, hullámos folyón.
> Hullámzik a víz, reng a könnyü sajka,
> Reng, mint a bölcső, melyet ráncigál
> Szilaj kezekkel a haragvó dajka.
> Sors, életemnek haragos dajkája,
> Te vagy, ki sajkám ugy hányod-veted,
> Ki rám zavartad fergeteg módjára
> A csendriasztó szenvedélyeket.

I'm a boatman on a wild, storm-tossed river; / The waves toss, the light boat shakes, / It shakes like the cradle that is rocked / By the violent hands of an angry nurse. / Fate, the angry nurse of my life, / You toss and turn my boat, / You, who like a storm drove on me / Peace-disturbing passions. (436)

Throughout the poem, the allegory and the autobiographical are united, yet the effect is not disturbing. The mysterious sounds the speaker hears are identified as the sweet song of a swan in flight and this inspires a sigh: "Oh fly slowly and sing long, / My dying swan, beautiful memories!" The next ten stanzas trace the happiness of boyhood before vague wishes drove him to seek solitude and the "fairy figures of his heart" bewitched him, drawing him toward ever disappearing goals just like the figures of the fairy tales.

The wished-for vision finally seems attainable on a bright spring day as he stands upon a mountain peak gazing into the blue sky. But, as he leaps to gain it, he is pulled back and faints. Returning to consciousness, he sees the vision:

> Meg mertem végre nyitni ajkamat,
> S beszéltem üdvről, angyalokrul, egről.

Nagyon homályosan beszélheték,
Mert ő nem értett semmit e beszédből.
"Én lyány vagyok," szólt, "földi lyány nem angyal. . . ."

Finally I dared to open my lips / And spoke of salvation, angels, the heavens. / I must have wandered in my speech / For she understood none of this. / "I am a maid," she said, "an earthly maid, no angel." (440)

And so the idyll is again returned to reality. Still, its progress—their conversation, their first kiss that seems to change the world—returns the poem to the fairy mood:

Alkonyodék. Arany felhőkön szállott
A nap violaszín hegyek mögé.
A messzeségbe nyúló rónaságot,
E száraz tengert, halvány köd födé.
A szikla, melyen állottunk, piroslott
A vérsugártól, miként bíbor párna
A trónon. De hisz trón volt ez: mi rajta
A boldogság ifjú királyi párja.

Dusk approached. On golden clouds / The sun settled behind the violet mountains / A pale fog covered this dry sea, / The endlessly stretching plain. / The cliff on which we stood glowed red / From the last rays, like a purple pillow / On a throne. But truly, this was a throne / And we on it the youthful royal couple of happiness. (444)

The affair lasts through the spring and the final stanzas recount the tearful parting. The poet's real regret, however, is not for the lost love—those wounds have long ago healed—but for the loss of the memory of this "fairy dream."

In a sense, this poem was a swan song. Petőfi was not to return to such purely internal lyric because, in the coming years, he was to be more and more concerned with the practical application of the poet's talent. Social and political problems intruded, even claiming a place in his love poetry. Appropriately, though, this swan song exhibits the best qualities of the subjective, romantic Petőfi. It is melodious; it unfolds the story in a series of rich and sensuous images that help to move events by their associations. The objective world is totally subordinated to the imaginative one, but it is not ignored. Like Keats' "The Eve of St. Agnes," the poem draws the reader into a rich and sensuous world that is quite real, although we know it exists only in the imagination.

Symbols abound. The identification of the girl with poetry is obvious, but does not exclude other interpretations. She is Imagination and Inspiration also; she is the ideal goal of those starting their careers. In her loss, the ideal is lost, but Petőfi suggests in the closing lines that such an ideal can only be held for a moment. It must give way to reality; thus, it is not lost, only changed. The impractical dreams of youth are supplanted by the practical programs of adulthood which will implement these goals. The poet, setting out on a practical program, regreted the sweetness of these half-forgotten dreams; but knew that this, the course of nature, must be run before the next step could be achieved.

III *A Confident New Voice*

Other poems written in 1846 show that Petőfi turned away from fantasy in order to devote attention to the positive programs he saw as steps in achieving his ideals. By the late summer he had overcome his depression, and his new style had evolved more clearly. The positive aspects of the poems of these eighteen months won out, and he consciously turned to the new style. The poems that were to follow, whether love poems, songs, genre pictures of landscapes, narrative, or patriotic poetry, demonstrated that he had reached the peak of his poetic powers in the three years before his death. Whether a new style would have supplanted this after the defeat of Világos, or whether he, like so many other poets, would have become mute under the tragedy, is idle speculation.

The epistle to his friend, "Levél Várady Antalhoz," began in a playful and teasing mood. He admits that the months spent in the country with his parents have cured him of his world-weariness and melancholy. The beauty of nature has revived him: "I am reborn! . . . No longer do I hate the world" (516). While he remained angry with society for tolerating injustice, he no longer wished to brood on the evils of society, but anticipated better times: "I begin to trust that soon the dawn of glorious days will come" (516). The last section, however, outlined a wish for revolution. It suggested the coming of a day of reckoning when the deprived and downtrodden of the earth would rise and wash all evil away in a new deluge of blood.

Petőfi had read Shelley and seemed to follow the more violent poetry of the Englishman here, not the ultimate solution he offers in *Prometheus Unbound.* However, this cleansing blood-bath, Petőfi indicated, would lead to the establishment of a new social order. Henceforth the poems which proclaim a revolution to eradicate tyranny and establish the universal rule of Liberty become important. Petőfi's role in the creation of the new order of things was expressed in "Sors, nyiss nekem tért" ("Fate, open the path for me") in which he called on fate to assign him an active role in bettering the lot of humanity. He sought to put into action the sentiments which had inspired him, even if this meant a martyr's death.

"Dalaim" ("My Songs") was both an expression of what his poetry was and what he intended it to be. In six stanzas Petőfi presented the varied moods of his soul as well as the type of poem each gave birth to. The dactylic lines reflect the cadences of speech and set a meditative mood without being in the least dark or brooding. Couplet rhyme, supported by assonance, gives orderly repetition of sounds throughout the poem and the last two lines of each stanza, forming as they do an incremental re-frain, further enhance the musical pattern.

The poet progresses from a dreamy meditative state to the im-patience of the reformer, varying the tempo of the poem ever so subtly to suit each new mood. In the first stanza, Petőfi suggested that when he contemplates the landscape of his homeland, his poems are "Moonbeams of my dreaming soul." This mood often gives way to lightheartedness: instead of worrying about the future, he turns to his poems, "the butterflies of my careless soul." Should he meet with a pretty girl, he forgets in her eyes all care, and the songs "born of these moments, / Are the wild roses of my amorous soul." Now, the tempo has noticeably increased, and whether the girl returns his love or not, he drinks in joy or sorrow and his songs become "Rainbows of my intoxicated soul." At this point, he is only a step away from considering the fate of his country: the tradition of the Hungarian anacreontic is closely allied with the patriotic, as his own "Egri hangok" had shown: Thus, he continues:

Oh de míg a pohár van kezemben,
Nemzeteknek keze van bilincsben:
S amilyen víg a pohar csengése,
Olyan bús a rabbilincs csörgése.

Oh, but while a glass is in my hand / The hands of nations are in chains; / And merry as is the ringing of the glass / So sad is the clanking of the chains. (496)

The songs of these moments are "Clouds of my sorrowing soul," and he is brought into a fiery rage by the contemplation of injustice, so that his songs become "Lightning flashes of my angry soul."

With this poem, the third and final phase of Petőfi's poetry began, though it also served as a bridge between the earlier and the later poems. The final period of Petőfi's poetry exhibits a harmonious fusion of the two often divergent trends of the earlier years, and seems to owe as much to his actual experiences as to his stylistic experimentation.[7] An intensely personal poet, Petőfi always sought the inspiration of his poetry in his life, and at this point in his career three dominant interests—romantic love, love of nature particularly as manifested in the Hungarian countryside and ideas of reform and revolution—became closely intertwined in both his life and his poetry.

The structure and mood of Petőfi's poetry, always dependent on the fusion of the external and the inner scene, from now on showed an even closer connection.[8] Furthermore, his themes became more complex and the subjects more serious. The "naive realism" of his early folksongs and lyrics was supplanted by a deeper realism. Objective observation dominated, and instead of personal comments, universal truths were stressed. In many poems the "I" was a "poet-philosopher," the political reformer, or the champion of national liberty. His "folksongs," too, became vehicles of his revolutionary ideals, following the conviction he had expressed in a letter to János Arany.[9]

Petőfi used forms that required a restrained style and made them carry intense feelings; yet he kept the balance between form and content. Nature, love, patriotism—the themes of the folksong—merged in Petőfi's love poetry at this time, as his wife became the center of his life and his love for her became inseparably united to his devotion to the cause of Hungary's independence and the freedom of all nations.

Hungarian criticism had labeled this period of Petőfi's career as the "népi-nemzeti," or "populist-national" era, thus differentiating it from the so-called "national" romanticism of Vörösmarty and his school. The division is too violent and does injustice to both schools. What really happened was a development of the earlier poet's ideas in the work of Petőfi and his contemporaries. Petőfi was the first to turn from the contemplation of past glories to a more positive and progressive program; he was also the first to present peasant life realistically, not through the idealized pictures of all romantics, Hungarian or otherwise.

The results of this fusion can be seen in the poems of 1847–1849. The explanation of its success lies in the earlier poems. Petőfi was able to recognize the limitations of both his models and of his own early verses without repudiating either; thus he was able to build on these earlier achievements to create a poetry suited to the times. While respecting the traditions of the 1820s and 1830s, he forged a style for the 1850s. In moving away from the dream vision of "Tündérálom," in recognizing the validity of many poetic moods, in emphasizing realism based on psychology rather than externals, he prepared himself for the compact poems of these last years.

CHAPTER 4

Júlia Szendrey

I *The First Meeting*

AT this point, when he needed a catalyst to bring his poetic style to new heights, Júlia Szendrey entered Petőfi's life. The emotions this experience awoke, even when not directly related to his poetical program, seemed to strengthen it. He had finally found a person who not only seemed worthy of his most lavish praises, but who could inspire even deeper emotions. And, unlike so many others, she returned his love.

Interestingly enough, the emotional experience did not lead to the deepening of the poet's subjectivity but rather to a flowering of his "objective" lyrical style. Perhaps this was because Petőfi was firmly convinced that a poet had a duty to society just as a husband had a duty to his wife. The two could only be reconciled if he not only supported his family through his pen but also assured himself a respected position. His youthful quest for glory was thus reenforced.

Petőfi wrote approximately 120 poems to Júlia[1] both before and after their marriage, and published almost all of them. He also wrote narratives, both in prose and verse, that celebrate the pleasures of a home adorned by a wife and children. Yet, his feelings were passionate and intense; he fell in love on first seeing Júlia and allowed nothing to deter him from his quest.

These love poems are, as a group, far superior to his earlier ones; the ones written after his marriage, however, are unique in their beauty and sincerity. Specific events inspired the poems, so it is possible to trace their courtship and marriage, the birth of their son, and even their last farewell in them. Of the several written after the first meeting, "Szerelmes vagyok én" ("I am in Love") shows the emphasis on the girl's physical beauty as merely a reflection of her spiritual characteristics. In "Te vagy, te vagy, barna kislány, ("It's You, It's you, Brunette Lass") he confirmed this: she was his only hope of happiness in this life or the next. When they are separated, he enriches his reveries with her presence, as he expresses in the melodious "Kellemetlen Őszi reggel" ("An Unpleasant Autumn Morning"). Confined to his room by the rain "Falling on the / Faded autumnal scene," he sent his soul to his loved ones: his parents and to a young girl he had met:

Járd be őket,
Járd be sorra,
S jőj meg késő est felé
Édességgel
Megterhelve
Mint virágokról a méh.

Visit them, / Visit them in turn / And return in late evening / Laden / With sweetness / Like the bee from the flowers. (553)

Dividing the "eights" into its two parts, and using its truncated version, the "sevens," he achieved a variety in meter that was light yet close to the cadences of speech. This rhythmic pattern allowed him to vary the tempo by the arrangement of the unstressed syllables: the last line is the slowest line of the poem.

The imagery of these poems also reflects his mature style. In the first one, the girl's soul is likened to a white dove, which is in turn associated with the Holy Spirit so that the conventional metaphor becomes a strong statement of his adoring attitude, as well as a means of leading into the "blessing" he wishes from her. The second poem evokes a sad mood by its reference to the weeping willow and the briefness of love and life that it suggests. The faded autumn scene, deserted by the birds, suggests another of the traditional symbols of transience. All of these associations are exploited in the third poem: the falling rain, the loneliness that hangs on the poet like a millstone set the depressing mood that is effectively contrasted by the sweet, rich, nourishing nectar that the remembrance of his loved one brings.

The poems to Júlia are characterized by a wide range of moods and styles: almost every one has a unique touch, which is not surprising since each is the product of a particular moment of emotion. They range from songs to dithyrambs, from the lyric to the elegiac, from regular to free rhythms, from rhymed verses to unrhymed ones. Something of the poet's scope is clear in "Reszket a bokor, mert" ("The Bush Trembles, Because"), in which the intensity of feeling is almost too much for the classic folksong pattern, yet the poet retains the delicate balance between form and content.[2] Petőfi wrote this in the winter of 1846–1847, in Pest, and it expresses the ever-recurring fear of those months that Júlia might no longer love him. The complex ideas are phrased in a deceptively simple verse in which each statement opens a range of associations:

Reszket a bokor, mert
Madárka szállott rá.
Reszket a lelkem, mert
Eszembe jutottál,

The bush trembles, for / A little bird alighted there. / My soul trembles, for / You came to my mind. (560)

The nature parallelism of the four lines, characteristic of Hungarian folklore, associates the beloved with the little bird whose presence brings beauty and song. More importantly, the repeated "Trembles" (in the original, the first word in lines one and three) shows the power she has on the poet. Then, in the concluding four lines of this first stanza, the poet summarizes all that she meant to him in similarly rich conceits:

Eszembe jutottál,
Kicsiny kis leányka,
Te a nagy világnak
Legnagyobb gyémántja!

You came to my mind, / Small, little girl, / You, the greatest diamond / Of the great world! (560)

The contrast of her smallness, her daintiness, and the immensity of her meaning to the poet is suggested rather than clearly stated; yet it is unmistakable. The imagery, too, becomes more elaborate: she is a diamond, therefore pure and clear as well as the most precious of all things.

The second stanza resumes the nature imagery:

Teli van a Duna,
Tán még ki is szalad.
Szivemben is alig
Fér meg az indulat.
Szeretsz, rózsaszálam?
Én ugyan szeretlek,
Apád-anyád nálam
Jobban nem szerethet.

The Danube is full, / It might even flood. / In my heart also / The emotions can scarcely be held. / Do you love me, my rose? / I do love you; / Your father, your mother / Cannot love you more. (560)

Again, the balance between the exterior, natural scene and the interior, psychological one is kept. The fullness of the river, ready to burst its restraints and spread over the countryside (though not in a dangerous or destructive way) aptly captures the fullness of the poet's own heart. He is no more able to contain his abundance of love than the river is its waters. Furthermore, the metaphor used for the girl, "rózsaszál"—not merely a rose but a single rose—suggests gracefulness and uniqueness in addition to the softness and fragrance associated with the rose itself.

The last stanza, which no longer uses the explicit nature parallels, poses a question: does Júlia still love him now, in the cold of winter, as she had loved him in the warmth of summer? The contrast of summer and winter, reflecting the summer of their love and the winter of their separation, is suggested: the actual moment from which the poem springs is thus made a part of it. This gives the emotions both immediacy and sincerity. The plea in the final four lines, preceded as it is by a note of gentle resignation, is thus all the more effective. The key word "ezerszer" ("a thousand times"), given in the run-on line and out of the natural word order, receives all the emphasis needed yet remains a sigh and a wish. The low key of the poem is not disturbed:

Mikor együtt voltunk,
Tudom, hogy szerettél.

Akkor meleg nyár volt,
Most tél van, hideg tél.
Hogyha már nem szeretsz,
Az isten áldjon meg,
De ha még szeretsz, úgy
Ezerszer áldjon meg!

When we were together, / I know you loved me. / Then it was warm summer / Now it's winter, cold winter. / If you no longer love me / May God bless you, / But if you still love me, then / May He bless you a thousandfold. (560)

The three-three pattern (divided sixes) results in a quick, very regular dactylic tempo. The falling cadence still follows normal speech, but its regularity emphasizes the poet's mood. It is through the harmonies of sound that the poet achieves variety and emphasis. Rhyme, assonance, repetition, and a range of vowel harmonies and consonances give the poem its special effect. For example, in the first stanza, the repetition of the final word ("mert"; "because") of lines one and three emphasizes the momentum of these run-on lines. The predominance of front vowels, liquids, and sibilants also allows the lines to move smoothly. Furthermore, the repetition of the fourth line provides the bridge between the two levels of the poem: there is a slight change of meaning between the two lines, however. The sixth and eighth lines are also rhymed, as if to emphasize the folksong quality. In the second and third stanzas there is less repetition, and the rhymes follow a more regular pattern, with the variations of the word "love" generally receiving the emphasis of the rhyme or assonance. Júlia, who read the poem when it was published in February in the *Életképek*, wrote in answer: "A thousand times, Júlia."[3] This was confirmation enough for the poet, and from that time on, he seems sure of her love.

The poems written during the courtship are full of references to the effect the beloved had on his life. "Kit feledni vágytam" ("The One I Sought to Forget"), after a brief reference to his old doubts, conjures up the physical beauty of the girl but concentrates on the "richness of the treasury of her soul which / Plays in seven colors like the rainbow." Recalling the days of their happiness, he tells her that she has given him hope and purpose, consolation and rest in a life that had been full of wanderings and vicissitudes. Then, aware of all she has to sacrifice for their love, he assures her that their happiness will make it all worth while.

II *Engagement and Marriage*

Once sure of Júlia's feelings, Petőfi's poems began to show a concern for her position in loving a man whom her father and her own society opposed. The contrast in their stations, on which this opposition was founded, was the theme of the proposal "Hozzám jösz-e? ("Will You Marry Me?"). Júlia's ability to give him all that he would want was celebrated in "Te az enyém, én a tied" ("I am Yours, You are Mine"), and the perfection of their love in "Hol a leány, ki lelkem röpülését?" ("Where Is the Girl Who Can Follow My Soul's Flight?"). The joyous songs of this time recorded the major events of his life. "Bírom végre Juliskámat" ("At Last I Have My Júlia") is an exclamation of amazement that she is finally, officially, his fiancée. He only regrets that autumn is still several months away, and then only would *his* spring come. In the meantime, he could not even anticipate his happiness, for its brightness would dazzle him. He will, instead, remember the fire kindled by their first kiss because his love will even warm his heart in the grave.

"Augusztus 5. én" ("On August 5") is a similarly breathless exclamation of joy as he contemplates the ring, sign of their betrothal, on his finger:

Itt a gyűrű, itt a gyűrű,
Itt van végre ujjamon!
Itt van ajka, itt van ajka,
Itt van végre ajkamon!

Here's the ring, here's the ring, / Here, on my finger, finally! / Here her lips, here her lips, / Here, on my lips, finally! (681)

In the next six stanzas he describes the effect of their kiss in imagery that ranges from the dawn to heavenly nectar and rapture which carried him to the skies. The piling up of images, reflecting the fullness of his emotions, was characteristic of his love poetry: it was as if the poet were at a loss for words, unable to find the image that expressed the essence of his thought. But it was really this richness that best expressed his sentiments. The metaphors, for all their great range, follow a progression that is believable in terms of the poem.

Some of the more meditative poems of this period deserve attention also. In "Múzsám és menyasszonyom" ("My Muse and My Bride") Petőfi set up a dialogue between himself and his "old love," poetry. The free-verse poem began in a rather light vein: the exchange between the poet and a female visitor who claimed to have been an old love. However, when she revealed her name, he asserted that he will not be unfaithful to his muse and knows that his new, human lover will not resent his first allegiance. Even though Petőfi's faithfulness to his career as a poet and revolutionary author meant financial hardships, Júlia seemed to accept this. Petőfi praised her again and again for her steadfastness and understanding.

The meaning of Júlia's love, particularly its ability to direct his life (and the freedom-loving poet was intensely conscious of this tyranny), was expressed in the epistle, "Válasz, kedvesem levelére" ("Answer to my Beloved's Letter"). She is, he states, the seat of the long-sought Godhead, and he will maintain himself worthy of the honor she bestows in loving him. If she wished, she could bring him to renounce his ideals, but he is certain she will never ask that. Rather, she will urge him to continue the career he had begun, and he will be sure not to besmirch the name he created for himself. She, however, should not go into the battle of public life—her role is to encourage and inspire, not to share his dangers.

For all the ardor of his love, Petőfi was aware of the difficulties he and Júlia faced. He took his obligations seriously: love for Júlia included a secure and happy home for her, children and domesticity. An agreement with Gusztáv Emich for his collected poems and later volumes of poetry, as well as his contracts with various journals, assured a minimal income. His friends, too, came to his aid. For example, Count Teleki loaned them his small, isolated castle of Kotló for the honeymoon.

The visit to Transylvania, the finale of their honeymoon, was a triumphant journey to this region of Hungary, then still administratively separated from the rest of the country. Petőfi was feted as a poet laureate, and he responded by praising the "Magyarness" of this region that had served as a bastion for the freedom of the rest of the country through the centuries of Turkish wars and the years of Habsburg domination. Before taking up their residence in Pest, the young couple stopped in Nagyszalonta to visit János Arany, the poet's best friend and one who was to stand by him and his family in the difficult days of the Revolution. The singular poetic relationship of these two men was united to a personal friendship of the two families that was to give Júlia the refuge she needed later, and allowed Sándor to be somewhat at ease when forced to leave her shortly after the birth of their son to resume his duties at the front.

One of the poems of the honeymoon, "Szeptember végén" ("At the End of September"), has justly been hailed as a masterpiece of world literature. Its three stanzas, in dactylic tetrameter, are meditative yet grand, suggesting that the poet's soliloquy is not just a personal matter. The images, however, are simple ones based on the scene at Kotló in the foothills of the Eastern Carpathians, and on the autumn setting with its associations of death. But, the atmosphere created in the first two stanzas is such that the conventional and even sentimental thoughts of the concluding stanza are lifted to extraordinary heights.

As if sitting in their garden, contemplating the mountains, the poet addresses his wife:

Még nyílnak a völgyben a kerti virágok,
Még zöldel a nyárfa az ablak előtt,
De látod amottan a téli világot?
Már hó takará el a bérci tetőt.

The flowers of the garden still bloom in the valley / And under the window the poplar still greens, / But do you see the winter world there? / Already snow covers the top of the peaks. (732)

The natural scene then leads to the psychological content:

Még ifju szivemben a lángsugarú nyár
S még benne virít az egész kikelet,

De íme sötét hajam őszbe vegyűl már,
A tél dere már megüté fejemet.[4]

In my young heart are still the flaming rays of summer / And in it still lives spring in its glory, / But see, gray mingles with my dark hair; / The hoarfrost of winter has smitten my head. (732)

The brevity of life, captured in a single expressive line that rivals Villon's "Où sont les neiges de l'antan?" introduces the next stanza:

Elhull a virág, eliramlik az élet . . .
Űlj, hitvesem, űlj az ölembe ide!
Ki most fejedet keblemre tevéd le,
Holnap nem omolsz-e sirom fölibe?
Óh mondd: ha előbb halok el, tetemimre
Könnyezve borítasz-e szemfödelet?
S rábírhat-e majdan egy ifju szerelme,
Hogy elhagyod érte az én nevemet?

The flower fades, life fleets away . . . / Sit, my beloved, sit here on my knee! / You who now rest your head on my bosom, / Will you not collapse over my grave? / Ah, say, if I die first, will you cover / Tearfully, my corpse with a shroud? / And can the love of a young man prevail / On you to give up my name for him?

The effect of these two stanzas, says Illyés, is akin to examining a rose: behind one set of lovely petals is another tier of even lovelier ones.[5] For example, the poet's melancholy is gently suggested; it is, therefore, all the more believable. The realistic touches about himself, and the exterior scene, further lead the reader to accept all that follows. Thus, almost imperceptibly, the reader is brought to the edge of the metaphysical. Aware that this area cannot be pushed too far, the poet concludes:

Ha eldobod egykor az özvegyi fátyolt,
Fejfámra sötét lobogóul akaszd,
Én feljövök érte a síri világbol
Az éj közepén, s oda leviszem azt,
Letörleni véle könyűimet érted,
Ki könnyedén elfeledéd hivedet,

S e szív sebeit bekötözni, ki téged
Még akkor is, ott is, örökre szeret!

If once you do cast off the widow's veil / Hang it as a dark banner on my headstone; / I'll come up for it from the sepulchral world / In the middle of the night, and take it down there, / To wipe with it the tears I shed for you / Who so lightly forgets your faithful one, / And to bind the wounds of this heart which even then, even there, loves you forever! (732–35)

The poet's control of his material, particularly his ability to charge the poem with intense emotion yet pull back just before it becomes sentimental, is well demonstrated here. The reader can feel with Petőfi, and at the same time experience the late September scene as a symbol of mutability.

Spring and autumn, promise and fulfillment, mingle on both the metaphorical and the real level here, and the expected coming of winter permeates both worlds. Petőfi suggests that life has no more durability than a flower, and that the only permanence mankind has is to be found in love, if that love endures beyond the grave. The themes of love, nature, and death are united in such a way that not one of them is slighted, not one of them is vague and impersonal. The technical achievements of the poem become unobtrusive in the expression of ideas that are intensely personal and yet universal. This is gained chiefly through the imagery. The metrical pattern, regular four-stresses in the twelve syllable line (quartered twelves), also supports the message. The predominantly descending beat of the poem is appropriate for its muted tones, and the rhyme (a b a b c b c b) emphasizes the progression of ideas within each stanza.

Though the married years were also years of increasingly greater involvement in public affairs and politics, Petőfi continued to write beautiful love poems to his wife. In "Rozsabokor a domboldalon" ("Rosebush on the Hillside") he returned to the happy, carefree tones of the folksong as he compared his wife's leaning on him to the wild rose bush hugging the hillsides. His joy was similar to the sun's "joyful trembling" on the waves of the Danube. Then, still in the light tones of the folksong, he attested that, contrary to rumor, he is not a godless man: even now he is worshipping his idol as he listens to her heartbeat.

In January, 1848, he wrote "Minek nevezzelek?" ("What shall I name you?"), seeking answers to the question he could not quite answer: what does his wife mean to him? Again, the images in their colorful richness tumbled from his lips, yet they seemed inadequate expressions of his wife's essence: her eyes are the evening star whose rays mingle with the sea in infinite love; her glance is a dove whose soft wings bring peace and contentment; her voice is the bell that awakens the trees which mistake it for the nightingale; her lips burn with the fire of the ruby and encompass the world in their eternity. She is, in short, both the mother of his happiness and its enchanted daughter, and all of his wild hopes and more marvelous reality, his soul's only the inimitable treasure: "sweet, lovely, young wife."

Similarly, in the poem written shortly before his death, "Szeretlek, kedvesem" ("I Love You, My Dear"), he gave a breathless profession of love in eighty lines. In free verse that ranged between lines of two and four stresses, he listed both the beloved's physical attributes and her spiritual and emotional beauties. He loves all her moods, her virtues and her faults. He loves her "As deeply as a man / Is capable of loving" (1–28), and he attempts to put into words why and how she has become his entire world, concluding with the refrain-like: "I do love you / As no man has ever / Loved anyone" (29–56). He is everything to her, but in return she is also his all, and all other relationships are lost in this love:

> Szeretlek szivemmel,
> Szeretlek lelkemmel,
> Szeretlek ábrándos
> Őrült szerelemmel!

I love you with my heart, / I love you with my soul, / I love you with my dreaming / Mad love. (1078)

The final tribute, however, is that he has learned all of this love from her.

III *The Idyll of Married Life*

The lyrics of Petőfi all confirmed his happiness with Júlia, and his narrative works reflected the same contentment. The idyll, "Bolond Istók" ("Crazy Steve"), probably best illustrates his optimism and determination to make the best of things. Written in the early months of his marriage, it is partly autobiographical. In its portrayal of the wandering hero who eventually found a loving wife and a safe haven, many of Petőfi's own experiences could be found. However, its objectivity, its restrained style, and its use of the scenes of peasant life counteract the aspects of a self-portrait. On the other hand, the poet's realism, humor, and keen eye for details made the poem what János Horváth called "the narrative masterpiece of Petőfi's lyrical maturity."[6] Petőfi experimented with metrics, and used a line that ranged widely in length, but tended to have three stresses. The result is a loose, short, and flexible form which he modulated to suit the mood and content of the narrative.

The hero, caught by a storm on the prairie, is presented as a wandering student with an irrepressible sense of humor which helps him to cope with the harshness of his life: he addresses the rain playfully: "Which of us will tire sooner?" and then the free association of ideas takes over. The youth's words to the emerging rainbow end in the prosaic remark that the city is still far away—and the girls there will hardly be able to feast their eyes on him that night. Looking around for shelter, he notices a house that had once seen better days:

Gondolá is fiatal barátunk,
Hogy elért e tanya közelébe:
"A tatárjárasnak itt talán még
Mostanában volt csak vége.

De ha benn még mostan is Timurlán,
Dzsengizkán s az egész Tatárország,
Még ugyis belépek, lábamat
Vissza még ez urak sem riasztják."

Our young friend thought, / As he neared the farm: / "Perhaps here the Tatar conquest[7] / Has only recently ended. / But even if Tamerlaine's still here / And Ghengis Kahn and all of Tataria / Even so, I'll enter; even these lords / Won't scare back my feet." (790)

The old crone who opens the door is hardly civil, but the even older master of the house allows him to stay. Making the most of things, as Istók usually does, he regales the housekeeper with his gay chatter until he is invited to stay, first to dinner, then overnight. In his attempts to cheer the morose old man, he learns that his host experienced a life of disappointments and now wants merely to die. The optimistic wanderer, whose own life had been filled with hardships, reprimands him for having despaired. This deepest of sins is the denial of God, he says; that is why the householder has been punished. Still, good fortune comes to all in turn, so he should wait patiently. Such speech pleases the old landowner who invites Istók to stay on with him.

Just then a carriage arrives bringing a young girl who seeks refuge in her grandfather's house. Fleeing her father's plans to force her into marriage, she begs for protection; the son is sent packing by the father whom he had denied earlier. Istók, sensitive to the altered situation, prepares to leave, only to be detained. In the months that follow, the farm, once so decayed, flourishes under Istók's careful supervision, and the old house regains its former state. Only when he feels unable to hide his love for the maiden does Istók seek to leave again, but this time he is effectively detained by her own confession of love and the marriage that soon follows. The poem closes with a scene of domestic bliss: as snow covers the world, in the snug house on the *puszta* the young wife spins and sings as her grandfather and her husband play with the boys: "Outside, the winter storm howls . . . inside / The spinning wheel whirs and joyfully sounds the song" (812).

The narrative is told at a quick pace with ample use of dialogue and soliloquy so that the ballad effect established in the meter and *a b c b* rhyme is emphasized. Yet, there is also a great deal of philosophizing. Istók's stoic acceptance of cold and hunger, his firm belief that everything can be tried at least once, and his unfaltering faith that life will turn out well, show a side of Petőfi seldom seen. His ability to create a fertile farm where once there were only barren fields is a testimony on the value of work. Petőfi, however, did not preach; he remained outside the narrative. But his values, his serenity, his cheerfulness, permeate the poem and give it its most significant meaning.

In other poems, the various village types are also immortalized. "A Vándor" ("The Wanderer") is akin to "Bolond Istók," but here only the young journeyman's monologue is given: cold and hungry, penniless and barefooted, he thinks of when he will laugh at the wind as he sits in his little shop with a warm hearth, a wife, and a child to keep him company. Petőfi's portrayal of the basic "qualities of the people in their daily lives"[8] is neither sentimental nor frivolous. The poems show a realistic approach to life, even when the darker side of human existence is glossed over or ignored.

These early months of marriage were productive ones, and many poems reflect contentment and good humor. Even the occasionally satiric portraits of various village types are drawn with sympathy. The procrastinating farmer of "Pato Pál úr" represents the conservative gentry who allowed their possessions—and their lives—to slip away. The refrain, "Eh! there'll be time for that yet," helps to establish the caricature. The figure is one Petőfi had already introduced in "The Hungarian Nobleman," but here the satire is stronger and the poem more humorous. This effect was mainly gained by heightened realism. Instead of the exaggerated portrait of the earlier lyric, this poem concentrates on the details of everyday life: seeking a wife, fixing up the house, seeing after the fieldworkers and even his clothes——all of which Mr. Pato puts off indefinitely.

The role of this type in Hungarian society seems to have been intended as the theme of the unfinished *Táblabíró.* Only the first canto of this "heroic" poem was written, but it promised to pillory the county judges and similar old, conservative gentlemen who often misused their power and who generally failed to use their positions wisely. They were, however, not suited to be villains as their punishment usually followed as a result of their own laziness. Petőfi was aware of the obstacles these men posed to the modernization of the country: he seemed to have been unaware of the historical reasons for such dogged backwardness, namely, opposition to Habsburg schemes to streamline and integrate their varied possessions. Hungarian laws and traditions, as well as Hungarian interests, had often been sacrificed in the name of progress until by the mid-nineteenth century opposition had, unfortunately, fossilized.

There were many industrious men and women, though, and Petőfi drew their portraits, too. Both the journeyman and Istók welcomed work. "A Kisbéres" ("The Hired Man") is a busy, self-assured young man who drives through the village after the day's work to get a flower from his sweetheart. This gladdens him so much "he whistles such a pretty song, even the larks could learn from him."

"A Téli esték" ("Winter Evenings") also emphasizes the industriousness of the villagers that enables them to enjoy their leisure on long winter evenings. The opening verse describes the barren, frozen landscape and contrasts it to the beauties of spring. But though "the beauty and treasure of spring and summer" are only "pale ghosts" in men's memories, this is the time when life inside, "in the warm room," is beautiful. Here, the family gathers. The head of the house and his friends talk over old times, smoke their pipes, and drink the best wine of his cellar. The housewife serves them, while a young couple plan their future. Near the hearth the children play, engrossed in the business of the moment. From outside, the maid's song is heard as she prepares for baking, and the well squeaks as the coachman waters the horses. The sound of the Gypsy musicians is heard from afar, and everything blends into "a quiet, soft harmony."

The sense of prosperity that permeates the scene is based on the year's work: the tobacco, the wine, the grain are all the products of the farm, and the household deserves these rewards. Just as the soft blanket of snow covers the earth and allows it to sleep and be renewed for summer, so the people, too, must rest to prepare for coming years. This continuity of life, the eternal cycle of nature, is also suggested in the three ages represented and their preoccupation with past, present, and future.

CHAPTER 5

János Arany and the Objective Lyric

I *The Two Poets*

PETŐFI'S marriage had a positive effect on his poetry. It gave him an inspiration and provided the subject that, in his love songs at least, he seems to have been seeking. Furthermore, it expanded his horizons to include scenes of settled domestic life. In such social matters he was deeply conservative, and now he could write about the joys of married life not as an outsider looking in, but as a participant. The need to earn a decent living, too, spurred him to write more, and more varied, verses. But there was another factor in the development of a more objective stance in his poems at this time, and this was his friendship with János Arany.

In 1846 a heroic poem based on the exploits of Miklós Toldi, a legendary warrior and folk hero, was submitted to the Kisfaludi Társaság (Kisfaludi Society) for its annual prize. The author, an unknown notary from Nagyszalonta, lived in rural isolation on the Great Plains but Petőfi immediately sensed that here was a great poet. In the letter and poem he wrote to János Arany (1817–1882), the younger man greeted him as a friend and brother. Of the two epistles, the prose one is more reserved and serves chiefly to introduce the poem which was published in the *Életképek*, Jókai's journal and the one Petőfi was chiefly identified with now. The enthusiasm, however, is unmistakable:

My Greetings! Today I read *Toldi;* today I wrote this poem; today I am sending it to you. It will appear in the *Életképek*, but I wished to let you know as soon as possible the surprise, the joy, the rapture which your work awoke in me. Truly, folk poetry is the only true poetry. Let us strive to make it dominate. When the people will rule in poetry, they will stand close to ruling in politics, also; this is the task of the century, gaining this the goal of all noble souls who have become surfeited with seeing how millions are martyred to allow a few thousands to be lazy and comfortable. . . .[1]

The democratic sentiments expressed here are also found in the poem, in which, however, the emphasis is on the newfound brother:

> TOLDI írójához elküldöm lelkemet
> Meleg kézfogásra, forró ölelésre! . . .
> Olvastam, költőtárs, olvastam művedet,
> S nagy az én szivemnek ő gyönyörűsége.

To the author of TOLDI I send my soul / For a warm handshake, a close embrace! . . . / I have read, my fellow poet, I have read your work, / And great is the ecstasy of my heart. (586)

In the following verses Petőfi asks a series of rhetorical questions: Who is he who has emerged suddenly, like a volcano from the sea, and claims, all at once, a whole wreath of laurels while others gather the leaves one by one? Who was his teacher and where was his school? The answer, of course, is that the poet learned his craft from nature and, like a true poet, he uses his gift for the good of the people, consoling them and easing their burden.

On his part, Arany answered with a letter and a poem[2] that expressed his pleasure at having received the praises of one whom he admired and joy at finding a friend. He also asked Petőfi's opinion on writing a serious epic in the popular spirit. As could be expected, Petőfi's reaction was warm. He immediately dropped the formal address for the familiar one and urged the writing of the epic as soon as possible, only commenting that the hero should not be a king, not even Matyás.[3] He suggested Máté Csák or Rákoczi.[4] Thus began the close friendship and profitable association of the two poets.

Though the epic discussed here and in later letters was never written, Arany was to write several historical ballads, and Petőfi also experimented with this form. For a while both of them worked on a romance about Mária Széchy, the widowed defender of the fortress of Murány against the imperial forces under Baron Wesselenyi. Petőfi's *Széchy Mária* was finished in

1847. While not one of his more important works, it is an entertaining account of the way in which the baron won the lady's heart and her castle. Written in the Hungarian alexandrine, or the twelve-syllable line rhymed *a b a b c c*, it has an archaic effect that is heightened by the occasionally formal language, particularly in the speeches of the protagonists. The descriptive passages and the similes show the same control and vividness that is found in the shorter lyrics of this period, whether setting the scene or reflecting the emotions of the characters.

The literary collaboration was even more important in providing Petőfi with a critic to whom he would listen and whose views he respected. Following the example of Arany, he tried to write in a more objective vein, to place himself in the background and to present the scenes and the people of his poetry as they really were. In this, of course, he was also following the goal of literature he himself had identified: to make the people rulers in poetry. This view had been given in the preface to the first volume of his collected poems, *Összes verseim* (January 1, 1847), in which Petőfi defended his poems against the charges of stylistic irregularity. His poetry, he pronounced, was not based on Latin meters, but on ancient Hungarian ones. Since these were as yet only vaguely defined, poets had considerable freedom. However, he declared, "I have an idea of what it is—intuition leads me, and where they [the critics] accuse me of slovenliness in rhyme and meter, even there am I closest to the perfect, the true Magyar poetic forms."[5] As noted earlier, it was Arany who systematized this versification years later when he was an acknowledged critic, poet laureate, and member, later president, of the Academy.

A series of poems show the immediate influence of Arany on Petőfi. Most of these were written at the older man's suggestion, or while Sándor was a guest in Nagyszalonta. Arany had suggested that he choose some topics that would enable him to express his ideas without making himself the protagonist.[6] One such poem was "A csonka torony" ("The Ruined Tower"). This local landmark had served as a fortress in earlier wars and so became a symbol of lost liberty in the poem. Another was an exercise in fun: a humorous, playful poem to Arany's son, Laci.[7] The most significant one, however, was a poem on an old woman temporarily living in the Arany household since her own house had been destroyed in a fire.[8] "Sári Néni" ("Aunt Sara") shows the blending of the qualities of the lyric and the sketch that is found to some degree in all of Petőfi's objective verses.

Though the poem presents a lyrical impression—and this is reenforced by the metrical choices and the use of a refrain—the reader's attention remains focused on the objective description of the old woman who sits on the front stoop and sews—perhaps she is sewing her shroud. The many gathers of her skirt seem to have become the wrinkles of her face and the clothes hang limply on her. The description of age in terms of the old woman is poetic yet realistic. All of the images are appropriate to her: "Her hair is winter . . . it is like bleached linen, but tousled like the stork's nest on the chimney." Her sunken eyes and flat chest, and her seemingly motionless heart, are similarly described through apt metaphors from everyday life. The poet concludes with a lyric outburst on relentless time:

Vad, tékozló fiú az ifjúság,
Két marokkal szórja gazdaságát,
De jön apja, a zsugori vénség,
S visszaszedi elpazarlott kincsét.
Sári néni, hej, mikor kendet még
Sárikámnak, húgomnak nevezték!

A wild, prodigal son is youth; / He scatters with both hands his riches. / But his father, frugal old age, comes / And retrieves his squandered treasures. / Auntie Sari, hey, when you were still / Called Sally, my little sister Sally. (644)

The last two lines, the refrain, give the poem a poignancy and a lyrical quality that the otherwise objective and even brutally truthful description would not reach. These also serve as a commentary on the passing of time and the old woman's peaceful acceptance of it. Old age was as much a part of the world of Petőfi as youth, and even in the early days of his courtship and marriage he remained aware of this.

II *Genre Scenes*

Petőfi's genre scenes, the descriptive vignettes of certain

characteristic aspects of Hungarian life, belong to the group of objective lyrics that the influence of Arany helped mold. Most of these poems present a generalized picture of the lives of the simple rural population. Petőfi portrayed the peasants and impoverished gentry who comprised the majority of the population, and particularly of the uniquely Hungarian population. City dwellers, the nobility, the agricultural laborers do not find a place in his poetry partly because they were not really part of the poet's emotional world, partly because they were still a real minority.

The poems center on the Lowlands, and its varied life. The *csárda*, of course, has a prominent place. This ubiquitous institution of the life of both the village and the *puszta* has figured in others of his poems, too. Like an English pub, the *csárda* served as a center of local activities but was also the refuge of travelers and the neutral meeting place of various segments of society. It was both a tavern and a hostel. The poem on the ruins of such a focal point of activity has been discussed; in "Kutyakaparó" ("The Run-Down Shack") and "Falú végén kurta Kocsma" ("Curt Tavern at the End of the Village") Petőfi presented contrasting pictures of the *csárda*. Like the majority of poems of this period, they are realistic. Petőfi refused to romanticize the scene. Unlike the German poets and their imitators, unlike even Lenau (whose Hungarian background gained him easy acceptance as a poet of the Hungarian Lowland), Petőfi saw the facts as they were: the tavern that only served sour wine, whose benches were swaybacked with age, and whose bed would invite no one. Even the hearth, so inviting in "Téli esték," was a wreck here: "Resting its head on one of its shoulders the chubby oven / Has its respected old visage covered by cracks instead of wrinkles." Naturally, the innkeeper and his wife are not much better. The outside of the inn is in as bad repair as the inside, and the only domestic animal around is an old hound. Even the surroundings are bleak: only sand and a few wild bushes are to be found. The sense of abandonment is aptly given in the concluding stanzas:

A harangszó a távol falukból
Meghalni jár ide,

S az eltévedt madár körülnéz csak
S odább megy ízibe.
Még a nap sem süt itt úgy, mint máshol;
Bágyadtabb sugára,
Mintha szánakozva tekintene
Ez árva csárdára.

The sound of the bells from faraway villages / Comes here to die, / And the lost bird merely glances round / And quickly goes on. / Even the sun does not shine here as elsewhere; / Its rays are tired / As if it were looking down in pity / On the orphan inn. (575)

The old stone saint who crowns the bare hill a few paces away provides the last ironic touch:

Ennek is valaki egy kopott tarisznyát
Akasztott nyakába,
Mintha mondta volna: menj isten hirével,
Mit állsz itt hiába!

Someone has hung a weather-worn / Old knapsack on his neck, / As if meaning to say: "Go, in God's name, / Why do you stand here in vain?" (576)

Realistic description, however detailed, was always directed to an overall impression: Petőfi did not indulge in an "art for art's sake" sort of cataloging. Here, the picture of the *csárda* was designed to show a type, and to show it in all its dreariness. Having spent many hours, many evenings in such inns, he did not romanticize them as foreign travelers tended to do. He took, instead, a piece of the Hungarian scene and presented it to his audience in poetic form, graphically and realistically. It is useful to recall here that Petőfi's audience was to a large degree unfamiliar with the scenes of these Lowland villages. The urban population and the better-off gentry, if they traveled, would bypass such places to stay with friends in comfortable houses or in the better hotels of the larger towns. If they did stop in a village inn, they seldom saw beyond the surface and noticed only what they wanted to see: a romanticized idyllic scene of rural life or an assortment of poor houses on a muddy (or dusty) street. Petőfi, almost alone among his contemporaries, and to a great extent even among his followers, saw the human element. He saw the discouraged innkeeper and his bitter wife whose surliness is surely understandable when even the sun and the birds avoid their habitation.

The *csárda,* however, was also the center of life and revelry. In another poem, Petőfi used it for his comments on the Hungarian character, although, like most of his poems, this too avoided preaching. "Falu végén kurta kocsma" is written in the familiar divided eights of the ballad and the folksong, rhymed *a a b b.* The language is simple and straightforward; Petőfi relates an everyday incident in an appropriate colloquial tone. The scene, established in the opening stanzas, includes specific geographical references. The little tavern is located by the Szamos, a tributary of the Tisza in northeastern Hungary (Szatmár) where Petőfi wrote the poem. Then, to enhance the vividness of the picture, all the inanimate objects and abstractions are personified: the tavern "kicks" the river and would see itself in it if night were not approaching. The ferry "is resting" and the darkness in it "is listening." Quietness pervades the scene.

In contrast, the tavern is really loud! The band is playing and the boys are shouting as they relax after their work. Having set the scene, Petőfi turned to direct statements in the ballad style with no words wasted in identifying the speakers. The speeches are typical: the young men address the innkeeper's wife flirtingly and request wine that is "old like my grandfather / And firey like my young lover." The Gypsies are encouraged to play because the young men feel like dancing even if they do spend their last pennies. The situation receives a dramatic turn in the seventh stanza as a haughty servant from the manor commands them to be quiet because his master wishes to sleep. In reply, the Gypsy is urged to play on—and the gentleman and his servant are both sent to the devil. When, however, a young girl requests that they be quieter because her mother is ill and needs rest, they put an end to the merriment without a word, finish their wine, and go home.

This poem has often been cited as one of Petőfi's masterful sketches of the character of the Hungarian peasant. As he had done in *János Vitéz,* here, too, he avoided didacticism or explications. He presented the scene, showed the way in which his villagers act, and allowed the reader to draw his own conclusions. This is a pattern seen in many poems. The diligence of old Sára, sewing in front of her house, the friendly evenings of good conversation and innocent games in "Téli esték," even the reluctant hospitality of the old gentleman in "Bolond Istók," all give glimpses of the real life of the Hungarian plain. Petőfi did not ignore the vicissitudes of the journeymen and wanderers, or the dangerous and sometimes exciting life of the highwayman, yet his poems leave the general impression that, among simple people at least, no one is refused shelter for the night or food for the next day's journey.

Two prose works, both written in the months after his marriage, develop these same themes. "A Nagyapa" ("The Grandfather") seems at first a romantic tale of innocence wronged, but it is told in flashbacks by the young man who made good in spite of all, who returned to his village to marry his sweetheart, and who prospered through hard work. The black and white delineation of rich and poor is not omitted, but the old man and his family do not ignore those less fortunate. As the old man concludes the tale, a beggar seeks shelter on the unusually cold night. He is admitted, and even when he reveals that it was he who had made the old man suffer so many years ago, he is allowed to remain. The family scenes are depicted with the same skill as in the poems, but here more attention is given to psychological motivations. Still, the style remains simple and lucid. In contrast to the generally turgid prose of his contemporaries, Petőfi wrote in the everyday idiom he used in his poetry.

"A fakó leány s a pej legény" ("The Pale Girl and the Ruddy Boy") is even more of a psychological study. The misery of the two ugly young people, their isolation in the community, and their gradual realization of the goodness each possesses beneath the unattractive exterior, is skillfully shown. These stories exhibit some of Petőfi's best prose style and abound in a subtle humor that makes them amusing but not comic. Petőfi was serious here, as he was serious in his poetry, but again he avoided both preaching and satire. Above all, the realism characteristic of his genre and landscape poems is a basic quality of these stories. Both characters and circumstances are believable. Unlike some of the early stories, which had been full of tales of revenge and implacable hatred (for example, "The Hangman's Rope"), these stories remain healthy and optimistic. The poet's reputation as a founder of modern Hungarian prose style, if based on these two novellas and his letters, is justly deserved.

III *Landscape Poems*

Petőfi's landscape poetry is also rooted in the life of the Hungarian plain. Whether a participant in the scene or an outside observer, he never considered Nature by itself but always saw it in connection with man. As a result, his landscape poems are mobile living pictures, not merely "paintings."

"Az Alföld" (1844), one of the earlier poems in this genre, seems to be an objective description of the scene in the tradition of the English and German romantics, but the reader soon becomes aware of subtle differences. First, Petőfi did not concern himself with individual scenes so much as with the essence of the entire place. Then, though he could be identified with the speaker and his emotions gave the poem its lyrical quality, Petőfi kept the emphasis on the external scene. He did not use it as a starting point for meditation, as Keats or Byron did, nor for moralizing like Wordsworth, but only to arouse a sense of awe and appreciation of the beauty of his favorite scenes. The comment, if given at all, is brief; it is not so much the author's comment as the expression of thoughts the reader has been led to, somewhat in the manner of Goethe's best lyrics.

The poem opens rather startlingly with a rejection of the mountains: the speaker can admire them but not love them, for his soul is on the "sea-smooth" regions of the Lowlands. Putting himself in the poem through a metaphor that enables him to rise above the plain and take in all of it at a glance, he continues: "My eagle soul is freed from its prison / When I see the limitless plains." From his vantage point close to the clouds, he surveys the smiling land that stretches from the Danube to the Tisza, and then begins to catalog the beauties of this region.

Stretching below him is an ever-changing plain, each aspect of which is presented as a scene in the endless drama of the

Alföld. Here, a herd of cattle comes to the well at noon; there, the galloping of the horses can be heard as they are driven by the herders to the accompaniment of loud shouts and the crackling of their whips. By the isolated farms the new wheat wreathes the scene in its emerald hue and the wild geese visit these fields at twilight. Deeper in the *puszta* the fringes of society find their place: the lonely *csárda* visited mostly by highwaymen on their way to market; the falcon who makes his nest in the aspen grove. The flowers, too, are wild and hardy: the feathergrass and the thistle give the lizards shade in the noonday sun. On the horizon, civilization can be seen in the line of fruit trees and the rising church steeples.

Though in the final stanza Petőfi became quite personal—he praised the land he loved, the scenes among which he was born and raised and where he hoped to die—the personal frame did not detract from the poem. It gave it a lyrical intensity that the objective description alone would not have reached. Also, the reader is not aware of the poet as a distinct person: Petőfi has become identified with the narrator, and the reader in turn also identifies himself with the speaker. Because each scene is full of movement, the reader is naturally carried by the glance of the poet from the grazing lands to the farms to the semidesert wastes of the *puszta* and beyond. In each scene, a moment in the life of the inhabitants, human or otherwise, is arrested. Then, as these move on, so does the reader, assuring the poet of the emotional identification of the audience with the material.

The metrics of the poem deserve attention because the subtle modifications of the "varied tens" are used to speed up or slow down the essentially dactylic tempo to suit the content. Each stanza has its own mood. In the fourth, for example, the slow movement of the cattle is reflected in the slower movement of the final lines where there are not only four stresses instead of the usual three, but also more caesuras, long vowels, and double consonants: "Delel*é*skor/ ho*sszú*/ g*é*m*ű* k*ú*tnál/ Sz*é*les v*á*lyú ke*tt*ős *á*ga/ v*á*rja" ("At noon, by the long sweep of the well / The double branches of the through await them"). Each of the underlined letters, or letter combinations, is long, and, though the stresses on *gémű* and *ága* are secondary, they still serve to slow down the line. The slight pause required between almost every word by the phonetic combinations also contributes to slowing the pace of the poem to reflect that of the cattle milling around the well.

In the next stanza, however, the meter is speeded up to reflect the thundering progress of horses. There are fewer long vowels and no long consonants, except for the double *ll*'s in *hallik* and *tt*'s in *pattogása*—both letters that roll off the tongue quickly. The only caesura occurs halfway in the second line, and the three-stress pattern is kept in each line. Finally, the *a b a b* rhyme, though often dependent on half-rhymes and assonance, reenforces both the quickening and slowing devices of the poem.

"Kiskunság," written in 1848 and one of the few lyrics of this period not concerned with either political or patriotic themes, presented the same region, but from a wholly different perspective. An air of longing suffuses it, for the poet was recalling the quiet scenes of the country when engaged in the activity of the city. He sets the scene in summer, in the heat of the noonday sun, when all creatures are at rest. Finally, the speaker is a traveler through the plain, not a soaring eagle, and so sees quite a different view. Petőfi chose a verse form that enhanced the meditative and conversational tone without allowing it to become either too monotonous or to close to the narrative tempo. This is a combination of six- and twelve-syllable lines, using two and four stresses respectively and a long, eight-line stanza with a complicated rhyme scheme.

Both herd and herdsman are resting. The water birds feed with measured majesty in the clear and mirror-smooth stream, but the well has long since been abandoned. As the traveler proceeds, he sees the *délibáb* ("fata morgana") which also seems to be resting: instead of fabled cities, it merely displays an old inn. By the farms the wheat hangs its heavy ears, and wild poppies, cornflower, and thistle lend the fields patches of color. As he approaches the city in the evening, golden clouds float gently above his head, and he stops to admire the windmills making cartwheel after cartwheel. This poem seems to demonstrate best the remark that for Petőfi "Nature was not merely a sight but an extended 'I.' "[9] Even though each of the scenes remains distinct from him and the poem is realistic to the last detail, the reader is gradually drawn to view the scene through Petőfi's eyes and feelings. The poet's mood dominates in spite of the seeming objectivity. This achievement is perhaps the key to Petőfi's artistic greatness. It is best explained by Petőfi's closeness to his subject and his command of the objective lyrical style he had developed.

A third poem on the same scene shows yet another mood and another scene. A winter picture of the *puszta* contrasts its half-dormant and barren exterior with the cosy life of the peasant in his cottage. Like the other landscape poems, "A puszta télen" ("The *Puszta* in Winter") uses the sun and the overall impression of the landscape as central motifs. The autumn, having squandered the accumulated wealth of spring and summer, has left only barrenness and silence. The clanking of the sheep's bell, the shepherd's flute, the sound of the birds, and even the chirping of the cricket is gone. Moving over the landscape, the sun, "like a tired bird," bends low as it seeks to see something. But there is no life to observe: animals and men alike have sought shelter.

The opening three stanzas are balanced by the three that show the animals peacefully feeding in the stables, the farmer filling his pipe and smoking the fresh-cut tobacco, and the quiet inns where the owners can sleep late, for no one willingly ventures outside in such cold weather. In the last three stanzas, the pace changes and the reader is offered a contrast to both the stillness of the opening lines and the peaceful mood of the middle sections by descriptions of contending storms, the pale mists of evening, and the lonely figure of the *betyar* riding to his night's lodging. The concluding stanza expresses the minor themes Petőfi had expounded in the poem:

> Mint kiűzott király országa széléről,
> Visszapillant a nap a föld pereméről, 7
> Visszanéz még egyszer
> Mérges tekintettel,
> S mire elér szeme a tulsó határra,
> Leesik fejéről véres koronája.

Like an exiled king from his country's frontier / The sun glances back from the edge of the earth, / He looks back once more / With an angry visage / And by the time his eyes reach the far horizon / His bloody crown falls from his head. (854)

Beauty and pathos, dying or dormant life—the aspects of the *puszta* captured here—are worked into both the images and the extensive personification: the seasons, the sun, the warring winds, the mist are all alive, yet there is something futile in their activity, as if they were going through remembered movements mechanically. Even the winds grow tired of their wrestling by evening and, wearied, "sit down."

"A Tisza" goes beyond mere description to turn the subject into a symbol. Through ten of the fifteen four-line stanzas the poet describes the river from the spot where he had stopped in his evening walk. From this seemingly narrow perspective Petőfi spreads a panorama before the reader, though again, the panorama does not exclude the human element. Furthermore, for all the plasticity of the scene, it is far from static: the poet had stopped "Where the little Tur[10] hurries into it [the Tisza]/Like a child to its mother's bosom." This personification of the river is retained throughout. For example, it flows gently, as it does not "wish the sun's rays to stumble / In the ripple of its waves" and the sand banks "march" toward the meadows. In the concluding stanzas, where the river's wild rampage at flood time is described, the personification becomes even more significant. This, however, had to be prepared for by the earlier references and the gradual "humanizing" of the river.

This poem also contains some of the most beautiful and most expressive of Petőfi's imagery. Each suggests a wide range of pictures to the imagination—scenes that can be developed from one clear image. The red rays of the sun, for example, are likened to so many fairies dancing on the river's smooth mirror, their steps almost audible as the jingling of tiny spurs. Often a phrase, such as the marching "sand-carpet," the fresh-cut hay lying in rows like "lines in a book," or the "silent majesty" of the forest beyond the meadow, carries some of this magic. The "rose-clouds swimming across the sky" bring memories of happy days but also direct the reader's gaze beyond the river's far edge and the distant town to the horizon closed by the peaks of Máramaros (a range of the Eastern Carpathians).

At the midway point in the poem, Petőfi shifts the imagery. This is appropriate, however, because the idyllic description is to be followed by a eulogy on Nature and then by an ironic reversal. The peaceful scene, consequently, has to be reenforced in the reader by sounds as well as by visual stimulation. Thus, the speaker notes the stillness of the evening broken only occasionally by the bird's song or the hum of a mill in the distance that resembles an insect's buzzing. A silent meeting with a peasant girl who has come to fill her water pitcher completes the scene.

At this point the poet seemed to enter the picture in an uncharacteristically subjective way to comment on his experience; the speaker is identified with the poet who stands transfixed, lost in a reverie:

> Oh természet, oh dicső természet!
> Mely nyelv merne versenyezni véled?
> Mily nagy vagy te! mentül inkább hallgatsz,
> Annál többet, annal szebbet mondasz.–

Oh Nature, glorious Nature! / What tongue would dare to compete with you? / How great you are! the more you remain silent / The more you say, the more beautiful things you speak of.– (592)

This digression, however, had been well prepared for. From the first, the reader had been aware of the poet. He was constantly reminded that he was seeing the scene not only through the eyes of a speaker but also from the poet's perspective: "*I* stopped on the evening of a summer's day; *I* stood; the clouds are symbolic of *my* happy moments, and the maiden looks through *me* as she hurries on." Furthermore, the personal commentary is sustained to the end where it becomes stronger. The two stanzas following it are a narrative account of the poet's return to the village and of his defense of the Tisza, "the world's mildest river," against its detractors. The climax comes a few days later when alarm bells arouse him from sleep:

. . . Jön az árviz! jön az árviz! hangzék,
S tengert láttam, ahogy kitekintém.

Mint az őrült, ki letépte láncát,
Vágtatott a Tisza a rónán át,
Zúgva, bőgve törte át a gátot,
El akarta nyelni a világot!

The flood! the flood! is heard, / And I saw a sea as I glanced out. / Like the madman who has burst his chains / The Tisza galloped across the plain; / Roaring, howling, it broke through the dike / As if wishing to swallow the entire world. (592–95)

The river Tisza, in many ways identified with the peaceful, productive, beautiful country through which it flows as it makes its way from the snowy slopes of Máramaros to the Danube, could suddenly become a raging monster. Petőfi turned it into a symbol, not because he made any specific reference, but because the river was expanded to include all that could be seen on the horizon or sensed beyond it. Thus, it was identified with the world of the village; it encompassed the poet's imaginative flights but also filled the girl's pitcher. It watered the meadows and orchards that gave fruit and bread to the men of the village, but also enabled the hazelnut and gorse to thrive and give shelter to the wild birds and animals. Thus, the river is Nature; it is Life. But neither Nature nor Life is forever peaceful. Petőfi, whose realism and sense of truth did not allow him to be blind to the harsher side of life, gave that its proper place too. The river could destroy as well as create, could kill as well as give life. And in neither, Petőfi suggested, should human motives be sought. Good and bad, peace and destruction are part of the plan of nature and man must accept both.

Friedrick Riedl wrote that in Petőfi's poetry "Nature is spiritualized and endowed with feeling,"[11] yet this is only true within the limits of the pathetic fallacy. Petőfi could be said to have "both felt and seen Nature,"[12] but he did not forget that Nature is neither benign nor malicious. It simply follows the rhythm of life—birth, maturity, death, destruction, rebirth. This is the pattern in all of the nature poems.

The genre and landscape poems are "objective lyrics." The poet, even when present, put himself in the background. Many are generalized statements, not personal confessions. But Nature, the scenes of his homeland, the bird's song, or the approach of autumn could also elicit a highly personal response. Some of these lyrics, for example, "Szeptember végén," have been discussed in connection with his love poetry. Others are expressions of different feelings: friendship, joy, grief, or the message of life amid the destruction of battle. Longing and homesickness is the chief emotion in "Szülőföldemem" ("On My Homeland"), a poem that conjures up the joys of childhood while it commemorates Petőfi's visit to the town where he was born. The mood is set in the first stanza not only through the words but also through the metrics: a slow, regular pattern of "tens" with a downward beat in which the long sounds are emphasized. The end-stopped lines and the rhyme scheme (*a a b b c c c*) serves to slow it down, and each couplet expresses a distinct idea or a separate memory.

The poem sought to recapture the carefree days of childhood and accomplished this by the concluding stanzas. The setting and the situation were unfolded gradually and the mood was set so that the reader is able to move backward in time with the poet. The refrain, "June bug, yellow June bug," suggests a pensive melancholy, yet is a children's song and lullaby sung by his nurse twenty long years ago—twenty years of sorrow and of joy. All the old playmates are gone, they do not come to help him forget the years. But his own thoughts "fly from place to place / Like the restless bird upon the boughs." As he gathers the many beautiful memories, "like the bee the honey from the flowers," he revisits all the old haunts and gradually becomes the child of five, whistling on his willow fife and riding on his hobbyhorse. By the sixth stanza, both the poet and the reader have drifted into the past:

> Megkondul az esteli harangszó,
> Kifáradt már a lovas és a ló,
> Hazamegyek, ölébe vesz dajkám,
> Az altató nóta hangzik ajkán,
> Hallgatom s félálomban vagyok már. . . .
> "Cserebogár, sarga cserebogár.". . .

The vesper bells are sounded, / The horse and rider tire. / I go home; my nurse takes me in her lap / As the lullaby sounds on her lips, / I listen already half asleep: / "June bug, yellow June bug." . . . (935)

The gradual progress of the poem, as well as the imagery and the interweaving refrain, all contribute to the emotional identification with the poet's journey into childhood. The matter-of-fact tone of the opening stanza is modulated in each, from regret to nostalgia, to curiosity, to the child's thoughtless joy and his carefree sleep. The rhythm of the poem slows down, too, with the vowels and consonants being used chiefly to express the slight modifications through the preponderance of long syllables in the final stanza.

The landscape poems and genre scenes, for all their objectivity, were not removed from the goal of Petőfi's poetic mission. They often shaded into social commentary because Petőfi continued to champion the common people as an important segment of the nation. The revolutionary and political poems of the last years of his life were to present a positive program; in these landscape poems he stressed the nobility and dignity of the people, their perseverance and hard work in both prosperity and disaster to make the whole country aware of their contributions to the life of the nation.

CHAPTER 6

"*Freedom, Love–These Two I Must Have*"

I *Poetry as a Tool*

PETŐFI's comments on the role and purpose of poetry clearly showed his belief in the mission of the poet. Even in the objective lyrics, he had a higher purpose than just the delineation of a scene or a picturesque way of life; he saw these works as political statements because they gave the common people a place in literature, to paraphrase his own comment to Arany. But there is a group of poems, supplemented by some prose works, letters, and diary entries, that give explicit evidence of his political and philosophical concerns. The critical comments on society in *Úti jegyzetek,* though couched in a light vein, already showed this involvement. His *Úti levelek,* more personal in tone since they record his courtship and marriage, also revealed his interest in the Reform movement. He was closely involved with the campaign to bring new ideas into the rigid processes of local elections, and he was generally accepted as one of the leaders of the Revolution. This role emerges clearly in his diary, a record of his ideas and activities between March 15 and April 29, 1848.

In the summer of 1848, following the establishment of a parliamentary form of government and the extension of the franchise, both Petőfi and Arany ran for office.[1] Though both were defeated in their home districts by the conservative candidates, Petőfi's campaign speeches and his comments on the victory of old-style politics showed that he was willing to work for reforms within the legal framework.[2] As yet, he was not a revolutionary, only a reformer. He was, however, beginning to see that the lack of idealism and dedication among the leaders might lead to the distortion of the ideals that had unified the nation on March 15. He sought the remedy in writing, hoping to educate the electorate to their responsibilities and to remind the elected officials of the important trust they held. On April 22, 1848, he urged Arany to accept the editorship of a new periodical in order to insure its retaining a populist national slant. Arany, who shared Petőfi's hopes for the role of poets in shaping a new social consciousness, was willing. He hoped that he could "speak to the people . . . because it is not such a secondary task to uplift the people slowly through literature that it would not deserve attention in the present times. I would like to be effective here; this would be my element."[3]

Petőfi, living in the capital and involved in the debates between the conservatives and the liberals, was full of hope at first. On July 1, 1848, he wrote: "How beautiful that future will be, my friend, how beautiful! You cannot imagine it; only I can know that for I see it as clearly as I see your portrait on the wall."[4] By August 16, however, he began to have doubts that this future could be realized without "a revolution which turns everything upside down but which also saves everything."[5] He felt the nation to be on the eve of this great revolution; if it should fail to happen, however, he believed the "nation would be lost, and lost so shamefully as no nation had yet been lost."[6] It is in the same letter that he announced the completion of his long narrative poem, *Az Apostol* (*The Apostle*).

Concern for the common man, a desire to make "the people" a ruling force, and a conviction that poetry had a vital role in achieving this can be traced in Petőfi's poems. As early as 1846, in "Egy gondolat bánt engemet" ("One Thought Troubles Me"), he had expressed the desire to die on the battlefield amid the blast of the cannon and the clash of steel, in the service of universal liberty. The poem's imagery contrasts the uselessness of a peaceful death with the violent death that he would prefer; such is the force of the metaphors, that the latter emerges not only as the nobler death, but also the more desirable one. The poem concludes with the belief that his cause will win, though the battle might be lost:

> Ott szedjék össze elszórt csontomat,
> Ha jön majd nagy temetési nap,

Hol ünnepélyes, lassu gyász-zenével
És fátyolos zászlók kiséretével
A hősöket egy közös sírnak adják,
Kik érted haltak, szent világszabadság!

There let them gather my scattered bones / When the day of the great funeral comes, / Where solemnly, with slow dirges / And flags draped in mourning / The heroes will be placed in a common grave: / All those who died for you; sacred universal liberty. (567)

Acceptance of Petőfi's responsibilities as a poet is a constant theme at this time, and therefore many poems are on death. This is not because of a morbid preoccupation, but because Petőfi was convinced that a man must sacrifice all that is dear to him if his patriotic and human duty demands this. In "Egy gondolat" the goal was still fairly vague; in "A XIX. század költői" ("The Poets of the Nineteenth Century") this obligation is stated forcefully:

Előre hát mind, aki költő,
A néppel tűzön-vizen át!
Átok reá, ki elhajítja
Kezéből a nép zászlaját. . . .

Forward, then, all who are poets / With the people through fire and water! / A curse on him who through cowardice / Abandons the people's banner. (581)

Furthermore, Petőfi stressed that no one is privileged to sing his private woes when the people need the "flaming pillar" of the poet to lead them to Canaan, the "promised land" of freedom.

Petőfi observed this rule in his own poetry after 1848: even poems on the most personal subjects (his son's birth; his parents' death) are not free from references to the struggle for liberty. For Petőfi, each action had significance only with reference to the Revolution: it might have pleased him to learn that it was this aspect of his poetry, this romantic-revolutionary aura, which caught the attention of foreign poets, notably Heinrich Heine, and Bettina von Arnim.[7]

There was a masculine quality in Petőfi's style which set him apart from many of his contemporaries who lamented existing evils but did little to remedy them. Petőfi always called for action. In "Ha férfi vagy, légy férfi" ("If You Are a Man, then Be One") he stated that a man must not allow fate to rule his life:

> Ha férfi vagy, légy férfi
> Erős, bátor, szilárd.
> Akkor, hidd, hogy sem ember
> Sem sors könnyen nem árt.
> Légy tölgyfa, mit a fergeteg
> Ki képes döntenti,
> De méltóságos derekát
> Meg nem görbítheti.

If you're a man, then be one: / Strong, brave and firm; / Believe this: neither man nor fate / Can easily harm you then. / Be an oak which the tempest / Is able to uproot; / But whose stately trunk / It is powerless to bend. (573)

The poet's insistence on the rightness of his unconventional metrical forms and his choice of the language of the people instead of fashionable poetic diction enhanced this masculine quality. Petőfi himself described his poetic fancy as the half-wild colt of the *puszta*, and in "Az én Pegazusom" ("My Pegasus") contrasted it to the English Thoroughbread and the German draft horse: his steed grew up in the open air, it had not been schooled but was caught half-wild by the poet. Even now, the plains were his favorite haunt, and he would easily bound out of this world at his rider's command. He would not tire until the limits of the poet's boundless desires had been reached. In this poem Petőfi gave his *ars poetica*: though seemingly unrestrained, his verses are carefully wrought, he suggested, for the rider is in control of his mount. But both horse and rider are uniquely Magyar, and they are dedicated to liberty.

In these last two years Petőfi was sure of himself as a poet and as a public figure. Only twenty-four, he could make his poems serve his goals. He was certain of his poetic instincts in both the choice of subjects and the metrics. In content, the poems kept stressing the necessity for all men to recognize the populace, the masses who had been so long ignored. But, he made them serve these goals without debasing it to propaganda. Although in these political poems Petőfi did not always avoid overt didacticism, or even preaching, as skillfully as he had done in his earlier lyrical and narrative poems, he could still develop an image to provide an objective lesson without neglecting its poetic qualities. For example, in "Vasúton" ("On the Railroad") he described the exhilaration of rushing along on a train at a seemingly tireless pace (stanzas 1–6). Then, in the last three stanzas, he suggested that the network of rails could be the veins that spread culture, education, and ideas all over the world.

II *Preparation for the Revolution*

Given his dedication to the people and his desire to be their spokesman, and if necessary their soldier, Petőfi's political and patriotic poetry is very important. As early as 1844 he was writing patriotic poetry, such as the "Egri hangok" ("Sounds of Eger") or the "Honfidal" ("Patriot Song"). But these poems were in the tradition of the early romantics: grieving, sentimental, dreamy. That was the fashion of the day, and great poets such as Mihály Vörösmarty and Ferenc Kölcsey had given the nation some memorable poetry in this vein. Petőfi, following the pattern, also relied on the contrast of the past and the present, and suggested comfort in the remembrance of past glories at a time when there seemed to be a slow decay of both the Hungarian language and of Hungarian traditions under the Habsburg bureaucracy. These poems were directed to the more educated classes, the gentry and the city dwellers. Nostalgic and sentimental, written in refined, poetic language, they reflected the tastes of the preromantics. The philosophical and historical reference also appealed to those classes whose political power had been severely curtailed and who felt it was time to assume a greater degree of self-government; the loss of national identity under the Austrian system was the chief theme.

By 1846, however, Petőfi had moved beyond this mood. He began to use the evocation of past glories as a starting point for criticism of the present, and thus to call for reforms. He came to demand the lost rights which other poets had only lamented, and he extended these rights to all men. Furthermore, he seemed to realize the need for political reforms to accomplish a thorough economic revitalization of the country. "Csalogányok és pacsirták" ("Nightingales and Larks"), for example, accused his fellow poets of being "nightingales," the birds of twilight whose song, no matter how heartrending or healing, brought no hope. He accused them of cowardice in their constant harping on the past, and went so far as to call them "grave robbers" who sought to resurrect the past which they have dug up from the grave. His own allegiance, he asserted, was to the future: he was the lark, the herald of the morning that was about to break. Though Petőfi seemed quite harsh in his criticism of these earlier poets, he benefitted greatly from them. The generation of 1790–1820 had established the foundations of modern Hungarian literature, and had awakened the historical and political consciousness of the nation. For these accomplishments Petőfi respected them; he attacked their successors who failed to keep abreast of changes and who were unwilling to make the sacrifices he considered important for the welfare of the nation as a whole.

Petőfi's patriotism was often most evident in those poems in which he adopted a critical tone. Naturally, few of his contemporaries recognized this, and he was attacked, especially by the conservatives. But, he continued to make his case and to call for reforms. At first, his program was vague: he suggested that liberalization of all ranges of activity—economic, social, political, religious—would lead to a state of general prosperity, He argued that much talent is lost when whole segments of the population cannot contribute fully. He took the nation to task for this, pointing out that many famous men had to leave Hungary in order to be recognized; many others never received a chance to develop their talents. He overstated the case, because opportunities for advancement did exist, especially through education, but it is also certain that between the conservatism of the counties and the economic policies of the Habsburg Empire it took an unusual amount of talent and perseverance to advance.

His use of historical references also changed slightly in the more positive, the more explicitly political poems. He suggested that Hungary should become the standard bearer for world liberty. He cited the Hunyadis,[8] János, who had stopped the Turks at Nándorfehérvár (Belgrade) in 1453, and his son Mátyás, the popular king who had curbed the power of the nobles and protected the rights of the commoners; the Zrinyis,[9] who had sought to protect the country from the Turks without surrendering its autonomy to the Habsburgs, and their descendant Rákóczi,[10] who had led an almost successful revolt against the Habsburgs with the support of the common people as well as of the nobility.

Thus, for all his criticism, Petőfi did not depart too radically from the traditional concerns of patriotic poetry. In his more objective and more critical stance, and in his concern for the whole of the country, he was more explicit than either his predecessors or his contemporaries; but, as he stated in "Magyar vagyok" ("I am a Hungarian"), he would never leave his country: "Because I love it, love it fervently. Even in its shame I adore my nation."

Such personal commitment was not enough for Petőfi. Again and again he urged his countrymen to be true to themselves and faithful to their legacy of liberty. Thus "Erdélyben" ("In Transylvania") is not only a lament for the separate status of Transylvania, the eastern third of the nation which had remained an autonomous district under direct Habsburg rule after the Turks had been driven out in the eighteenth century, but also a call for union. With his usual critical stance, he turned this meditative poem into a survey of the events that had led to the present state. The invocation established the proper mood:

> Barangol és zúg, zúg az őszi szél.
> Csörögnek a fák száraz lombjai,
> Mint rab kezén a megrázott bilincs.
> Halgass, zúgó szél, hadd beszéljek én!

The autumn wind roves and soughs, it soughs. / The dry foliage on the trees rattles / Like the chains rattling on the prisoner's hand. / Be silent, sighing wind; let me speak! (547)

He addressed the one nation that is two countries, pointing out that internal strife and jealousies had made this partition possible. The phrase "Had we but kept together" is repeated, refrainlike, to drive home the point that, united, the nation would have remained great and free. But, the long-lost union can be reestablished; it has only to be willed and "the awesome days that are to be born" will make it a reality. "Let us honor the fine, the holy handclasp" that will make the two countries one again, he reiterates at the end—and curses all who refuse it.

The union, so fervently wished for, was achieved in the days of independence, but it was suspended again after the defeat of Hungary until the Compromise of 1867. Petőfi, who was prophetic in many of his poems, seems to have sensed the events that were to come. Not only did he die on the battlefield, but in the very region whose union with Hungary he had worked to obtain and in which he had planned to settle with his wife and child.

Horror of prison and of all forms of subjugation is expressed in "A munkácsi várban" ("In the Fortress of Munkács"). Petőfi had gone to visit the famous fortress of the Rákóczis—which Ilona Zrinyi, mother of Ferenc II, had defended against the Habsburg armies—and found it being used as a prison. The refrain concentrates his fear and loathing of prison: "I could face execution bravely / But this is a prison—I fear it." The rejection of all forms of restraint was merely another expression of Petőfi's love of liberty, *the* essential element in his patriotism. Even as a schoolboy, he had found restrictions on his personal freedom chafing enough to denounce years later.[11] He could not give up his independence for either money or fame, as the relatively early allegories, "A kutyák dala" ("The Song of the Dogs") and "A farkasok dala" ("The Song of the Wolves") had expressed. The dogs rejoice in an easy life; their food and shelter is assured—but they must submit to their owners' whims. The wolves are cold, hungry, and constantly in danger from hunters—but they are their own masters; they are free. Petőfi praises the wolves and scorns the dogs, clearly indicating his preferences.

János Horváth, an early critic of Petőfi's, observed correctly that the poet was able to create a concrete reality from the abstract ideal of Liberty, partly because he always thought of it in concrete terms of national and popular freedom.[12]

Though some of his poems did speak of world revolution and universal liberty, his conception of this abstract idea and his framing of it remained rooted in the need for the nation, that is, the people, to achieve freedom. Civil rights and liberties must be extended to all classes, he argued in poems such as "A nép nevében" ("In the Name of the Populace"). This "alarm" poem or tocsin warned the ruling classes that all men must be assured certain rights because, if these are not given, the people will seize them by force. The poem mentions Györy Dózsa, leader of a sixteenth-century peasant revolt, as a warning of what the ultimate consequences could be, but gives more emphasis to the positive argument: it is the labor of the people which wrests wealth from the land and the mines, and it is their hands that must defend the country. In this early (1847) political poem, Petőfi posed possibilities and offered alternatives. He already considered himself the spokesman of the people, and he addressed those in power. He presented his message in the form of a warning, but framed it with a reminder of the power of the masses. This is the pattern found most frequently in such warnings, particularly those written in this year preceding the Revolution.

What had seemed, in these early poems, Cassandra cries, became prophetic calls to arms in the later half of 1848 and in 1849. The poet's forces and visionary power soon came to be recognized and appreciated. Though he could not change events, Petőfi's role in the establishment of a national consciousness during the Revolution and afterward cannot be denied.

III *Poet and Popular Leader*

In 1848 several factors came together that almost led to the new order Petőfi had been writing about. Undoubtedly, much of what seems prophetic in his poetry was really the sensitive poet's almost subconscious feel of the pulse of the times: he gave voice to the feelings, ideas, and aspirations that animated the public in the 1840s. The period of astounding activity and phenomenal changes which had been ushered in in the 1790s was coming to a culmination. Though there seemed to be few gains for the liberals, though life seemed to go on in its accustomed channels, there were very real modifications in society. An avid, if often nondiscriminating, reading public had been forged, and a sense of national pride was emerging even among the historically nonpolitical classes. Economic disasters and successes contributed equally to popular involvement in reform movements, and ideas from abroad, especially England and France, made many others eager for progressive changes. The diet of 1848, for example, debated many points later written into the constitution. Lajos Kossuth, by then out of prison and active as the leader of the radical segment of the reformers, was already working for the acceptance of his liberal platform.

Thus, even while Petőfi raged against the statesmen for inaction, there were men concerned with the introduction of reforms. Admittedly, they had to resort to compromise, to finding their way between the basic conservatism of many county delegates and the reactionary and imperial tendencies of the Habsburg Court. The situation remained delicate, since the king's consent was needed for the enactment of all laws, and this consent was in turn dependent on the nobles in the council. This group, however, not only opposed all liberal ideas in the spirit of Metternich and the Congress of Vienna, but also feared all nationalistic overtures. Thus, many reformers, Count Széchenyi among them, advised caution lest the court revoke all the concessions that had already been gained.

This situation was altered in the early days of March, 1848. The diet was still sitting in Pozsony while news of the revolutions in Paris, Italy, and Germany reached Pest. Even Vienna was caught up in the fever, and both the diet and the court had to take notice. Pest, though not a city with a large working class nor the seat of the government, was at the time quite capable of emerging as the leader. The concentration of students and writers was one factor. Its position as the chief economic and industrial city helped, as did the fact of its former position as capital of the country and the seat of both the government and the king. Finally, the annual fair had drawn men from all over the country and made the city, almost by accident, representative of the views of the entire nation. A banquet planned for Sunday. March 19, to be held on the Rákos meadows just east of the town, was to include the people as well as the students.[13] It was for this occasion that Sándor Petőfi wrote his "Nemzeti Dal" ("National Ode"), and it was this poem which served as a catalyst of the many segments of the crowds that, on March 15, seemed to sweep all opposition before them and to push through their reforms peacefully.

On March 15, with surprising suddenness, the students and young men of Pest saw the chance to urge acceptance of their liberal program by the leaders of the city and even the royal government in Buda. Petőfi's poetic interests truly merged with his political ones. By midday, the "Nemzeti Dal" was published as the first product of the free press. Going to the publishing house of Landerer and Heckenast, the young men had seized the presses and set the poem as Petőfi dictated it, then distributed the still-wet flyers among the crowds. This, along with the political manifesto quickly named the Twelve Points, was read again and again that day at rallies held in several parts of the city, until gradually even the various municipal and country authorities accepted the demands in principle, and released the one political prisoner held in Buda, MihályTáncsics, who had been jailed for the printing of an illegal (i.e., not censored) periodical.

Although the greatest fear of the authorities was that these demonstrations would turn into a riot and life and property would be endangered, it soon became clear that the March Youth, as Petőfi, Jókai, and their companions were called, was able to keep order. Considering the youth of the majority of the demonstrators, and the fact that among the countrymen many were herdsmen who carried weapons for their protection on the plains, or farmers who were also armed when they brought wares at a great distance, this is remarkable. The unity of the city, the lack of any real reluctance on the part of the authorities to listen, and the wise decision not to call out the troops, probably all had a part in this. In a matter of hours, news of the events in Pest reached the diet in Pozsony, and two days later, when the upper chamber was called upon to ratify the new legislation, Széchenyi could point to the orderliness of events up to that point yet suggest that, if angered, the Hungarian youth might also do what the Viennese had done, namely, loot and riot.

The Twelve Points, embodying both the platform of the liberal or opposition party of the diet and the demand of the students and all those associated with Young Hungary, were drafted by Petőfi's friend and fellow writer, Mór Jókai. They demanded: (1) freedom of the press and the abolition of censorship; (2) a responsible ministry in Buda-Pest; (3) an annual diet in Pest; (4) equality before the courts in civil and religious matters; (5) a national guard; (6) universal taxation; (7) the abolition of feudal burdens; (8) a franchise based on equality; (9) a national bank; (10) a requirement that the military swear loyalty to the constitution, the use of Hungarian soldiers within Hungary, and the removal of foreign troops; (11) the liberation of political prisoners; (12) the union of Transylvania and other military or frontier districts with the territory, administration, and government of the main body of the nation. None of these points changed the relationship of Hungary and Austria essentially; the principles were quickly accepted by the lower house. Even the signature of the king, Ferdinand V, was obtained on the bills that put these reforms into effect by April 11.

Petőfi, though one of the more liberal and more radical of the politicians, did not differ from the national-liberal movement in its philosophy. The young men of Pest, most of them under thirty, might have been impatient with the slow deliberations of the diet, but they were chiefly concerned with giving Hungary a modern government and modern institutions. The king, even a hereditary Habsburg monarch, was considered acceptable as long as he became a constitutional monarch whose edicts were countersigned by the ministry. In effect, the king remained the chief executive. Problems still remained—for example, compensation to the nobility for its lost privileges, the position of the national minorities, the conduct of "common affairs" shared by Austria—were issues which no one doubted would be eventually resolved.

What prevented the peaceful evolution of a new and modern Hungary was the partisanship of certain Austrian aristocrats who were not willing to see liberal ideas win out in Hungary lest this lead to demands for reform in other parts of the Empire, notably the heredity provinces of Austria and in Bohemia. It was they who fomented trouble and urged the Croatian Jellačiś, a fanatic Illyrian nationalist, to attack Hungary. The resultant war drove Hungary to seek complete independence. Yet, when after the bloodbath of the Bach era the Viennese government sought reconciliation, the March laws became the cornerstone of the Compromise of 1867.

In the heady days of March, 1848, both Vienna and Pest were seething with revolutionary ideas as the echoes of the Paris Revolution swept eastward. It was the ability of Petőfi to put into words the feelings of the students, clerks, small merchants, and tradesmen of the Kossuth to deliver these sentiments effectively that sustained even the Viennese revolt. But what differentiated the Hungarian Revolution from the others was that it was supported by most of the population. No one class was hostile to it as a body; the "political nation," that is, the nobility, supported it, even though some of the more conservative members were reluctant to grant all of the reforms overnight. The one large segment of the population which was not actively in favor of the reforms were the nationalities (but excluding the Germans who supported it for the most part); in most instances this was due to lack of interest. Moreover, since none of the laws dealt with the nationalities as a separate unit within the nation, the benefits of reform were naturally presumed to extend to all, regardless of national origin. When large masses of these nationalities, incited by foreign agents, attacked the country, Petőfi wrote angry poems, condemning the behavior of those who had benefited from Hungarian rule, who had the same advantages extended to them now as the others, yet who, in a pinch, had become traitors.

Petőfi, for whom the program of social reform and political independence were closely connected, believed that if social and legal reform were granted, the economic and national differences would be eradicated naturally. Whatever the precise facts were, Petőfi based his attacks on the not unsupported conviction that the only reason the Slovaks or Rumanians were worse off than the Hungarians was that a larger percentage of them were peasants, and few belonged to the relatively free peasants of the Great Plains.

As the good days of March and April passed, Petőfi became concerned. The court, feeling secure once more, put a new king on the throne who reneged on the solemn edicts of Ferdinand. The diet relapsed into its usual deliberative mood and seemed to dawdle. Finally, the attacks by Jellačiś were not repulsed forcefully enough. In poem after poem, the poet urged action. "Az országgyűléshez" ("To the Diet") scolded the lawmakers for their failure to grant the first requirement of a free state, namely, a free press. They were, he argued, like a builder who wishes to start with the spire of the church and put in the foundation last. But all around him he saw procrastination and empty debate that promised to choke the movement ("Megint beszélünk csak beszélünk"; "Again We Talk, Only Talk"). He invoked the spirit of Ferenc Rákóczi to finish the task he had begun, and to return to lead the forces dedicated to the triumph of liberty. Keeping close watch on events in Europe and the sentiment among the liberal students and intellectuals, Petőfi knew the importance of decisive action.

To a great extent he had been responsible for the mass movement that won immediate concessions from the authorities on March 15. As a leader of the March Youth he had forced through the suspension of censorship, the freeing of Táncsics, and the essential acceptance of the Twelve Points. In spite of the freezing rain that fell all day, he had kept the crowd of citizens and peasants on the streets until the desired promises were exacted. Several times he recited his "Nemzeti Dal" as copies were distributed among the listeners.

This spirited call to arms soon became the rallying cry of the nation and its ringing refrain,

A magyarok istenére
Esküszünk,
Esküszünk, hogy rabok tovább
Nem leszünk!

By the God of the Magyars, / We swear / We swear that captives / We'll no longer be! (888)

soon spread beyond the boundaries of the city. Petőfi united in this poem the nostalgia for the past with faith in the future. He emphasized the urgency and immediacy of the situation in lines that virtually leapt at the listener:

Talpra magyar, hí a haza!
Itt az idő, most vagy soha!
Rabok legyünk, vagy szabadok?
Ez a kérdes, válasszatok!—

Up, Magyar, the country calls! / Here's the time, now or never! / Shall we be free or captives ever? / This the question; you must answer! (888)

Appealing as the words and sentiments were, its metrical mastery contributed to the poem's success. The two-two pattern of eights placed the stress (generally) on the first and fifth syllables of each line, and at the same time gave it a quick rhythm which Petőfi enhanced by his use of monosyllabic words. The refrain lines, however, contained a variation: the one-stress, three-syllable line of "Esküszünk ("We swear") and "Nem leszünk" ("We will not be") alternate with the longer lines for an even more forceful pronouncement.

In the six stanzas of this poem Petőfi chided his countrymen for enduring servitude while their fathers cursed them in their graves. Anyone who draws back now, he thundered, is worthless because it is high time that the sword replace the chain. The Hungarian name, he assured his audience, shall again be great and their descendants will bless these brave men. The language and the images are as direct as the tone, and throughout the poet emphasizes the need for heroic action regardless of the consequences. Understandably, the poem had great impact. If Petőfi had made only this contribution to the Independence movement, he would have been remembered. But he did much more.

Petőfi's diary shows that he was among the most active, urging the other writers not to let this opportunity slip. He helped to draft the proclamations that were read to the crowds. He urged concerted action with the revolutionaries in Vienna; yet, at this time, Petőfi did not seem to have total independence in mind. He advocated the abolition of inequalities before the courts, in taxation, and in suffrage, but did not believe that the entire governmental structure had to be overturned to accomplish this. He saw the need to retain order[14] and helped form a Committee of Safety to insure this. Later, he became a member of the national guard whose first duty was to keep civil order,[15] since the foreign soldiers were either gone or were in the process of being withdrawn. He and his companions were quite aware that the reactionary forces in the Habsburg court would use the pretext of ensuring public safety to order in troops, and so they made sure to avoid any such pretext gaining credence.

When the attacks by Jellačiś were sanctioned by the new emperor, Petőfi became more revolutionary. In April, he urged an open break with Austria[16] and later he wrote the Jacobin poem, "A királyokhoz" ("To the Kings"). While earlier poems seemed to blame those around the king for abuses and merely suggested that the king is no wise ruler if he isolates himself from his subjects, here he warned: "Bármit mond a szemtelem hízelgés, / Nincsen többé *szeretett* király!" ("Whatever bold flattery might say, / There is no longer a *beloved* king," 898).

Of course, the poem was severely criticized, all the more so because the cabinet had hoped to invite the king, forced to flee a second time from Vienna, to Buda. The ministers still hoped that by keeping their ties with a world power they would insure the survival of the country. Moreover, there was a genuine reluctance on the part of almost everyone, in or out of the government, to allow the Hungarian movement to degenerate into a lawless orgy directed against all those in authority: the example of the French Revolution was more sobering than encouraging to all but a few hotheads. Petőfi, who distrusted deliberations and compromises, found these efforts dangerous. Unused to intrigue, he called for more decisive action. His speeches, his letters, his poems, become more militant. "Van-e mostan olyan legény" ("Is There Such a Lad Now?") is a recruiting song, one of the many war songs he was to write in the last year of his life. Some of these poems showed anti-German feeling, but most of them were glorifications of revolutionary and Hungarian ideals. He also celebrated victories such as the reunification of Hungary and Transylvania ("Két ország ölelkedése"; "The Embrace of Two Countries"). These months were not free of frustrations, however, and his bitterness and disillusionment were all poured into the long political narrative, *Az Apostol* (*The Apostle*).

IV Az Apostol

During the summer of 1848, while compromises were sought with the Habsburgs, the new laws were slowly and not always perfectly implemented. To Petőfi it seemed that the promise of March had been betrayed. Even among his companions he sensed an emerging conservatism. His defeat in the elections for the Kiskún district, and especially the virulent personal campaign against him, added to his disappointment. The poetic result of these months was the long narrative poem, *Az Apostol.* Though written in the summer of 1848, it contained ideas found in much of his earlier poetry. Here, however, these were concentrated in the heroic and tragic figure of Szilveszter who embodied much of Petőfi as he saw himself.

First, the poem affirms that resistance, even when futile, is noble. Still, it is an extremely pessimistic poem, because the victory of right is projected into the future, indicating that Petőfi had quite given up on reforms in his own time. The hero suffers and dies for his ideals, but instead of being honored, he is despised even by those whom he sought to help.

The poem, of over 3,600 lines, is divided into twenty chapters of irregular length. For the vehicle of his chagrin and disappointment, Petőfi chose a flexible style which allowed him to move easily from narrative to lyrical passages. The basic iambic rhythm and the varied line lengths suggest free verse, giving it both variety and naturalness. Almost never do two consecutive lines have an equal number of syllables, and this planned irregularity extends to the rhyme also: it is occasional and used for emphasis or to increase the lyricism of a passage. Thus, some speeches and descriptions seem to be songs set into the poem while others suggest meditative odes.

Into this poem Petőfi poured the thoughts of many years. Gyula Illyés called it "the dictionary of his principles" in which the meanings he ascribed to words like "happiness, liberty, God, priest, rebellion, tyranny, king" are revealed.[17] Within limits, this statement is true, but it must be remembered that the poem found its form in a very dark period of the author's life, and consequently only the dark side is shown.

The poem opens in the middle of the hero's career at a time when he is almost destroyed by anxieties over the future of his country. The opening scene, chosen for its emotional impact and thematic importance, shows the hero in the moment of decision: should he choose his ideals and bring death upon his loved ones, or choose survival, and compromise his dedication to liberty and humanity. By putting his learning at the service of the establishment, he would assure a comfortable future for himself and his family, but he would be untrue to himself and betray all of their former sufferings. While Szilveszter ponders this decision, the poet sketches the poverty of the little household in suggestive and realistic terms: a flickering candle reveals a damp garret room furnished only with a rough table and bed, some chairs and straw sacks. Here, the mother attempts to nurse her starving child while the older boy sleeps. The father, sitting at the table, is lost in thought, but when he has given the last piece of bread to the child and all the rest are asleep, his thoughts soar: he has made his decision, and he accepts his destiny: he will work to free his fellowmen and prays to God for strength. The reward he seeks is the happiness of others. With this, the scene closes and Szilveszter, too, sleeps.

In the next stanzas, Petőfi contrasted the gloom of the opening lines with the promise of dawn. There, the moonless and starless dark night made "the world as black / as a rented conscience." Here, the rising sun seems to crown the sleeping man "with a golden crown that is like / A bright, warm kiss from God's lips." The setting and the shift from hopelessness to the promise of a glorious future, as well as the apotheosis suggested by the sunlight streaming on the sleeping man, is an appropriate introduction to the survey of his life. The biographical flashback introduced by the question, "Who is this man, so haunted by fate yet seemingly blessed by God?" is answered in the following chapters (4–14).

Szilveszter, abandoned as infant, is found by a thief on

December 31—thus his name. He can hardly walk when his foster father begins his training in the trade, but when the child is only four, the thief is caught and hung. He would most likely starve, but a sham beggar, an old hag, takes him in to beg for her. In a few years' time, he is saved from a life of crime by a well-to-do gentleman who decides to take him home as a servant and whipping boy for his own son. Though in better physical circumstances, Szilveszter finds the young man's tyranny hard to bear. His only consolation is that now he has a chance to study; he therefore submits to the abuse heaped on him until his sixteenth year. At this time, a particularly unjust attack by the "young master" triggers a rebellion that can not be stifled, as he declares:

> . . . ha a lázadás az,
> Midőn az ember érzi és kimondja,
> Hogy ő is ember, mint akárki más,
> Ugy büszkén mondom: lázadó vagyok.

. . . If it be rebellion / When a man feels and says / That he, too, is human like anyone else, / Then I'll proudly say: I am a rebel. (chapter 95 p. 1004)

Though again without food or resources, Szilveszter's prospects are still not hopeless: the tutor, who had long sympathized with the bright boy, gives him money to complete his studies.

As he reflects on how best to invest the money so generously given him, Szilveszter decides to dedicate his life to bettering the lot of other men. Liberty, he knows, is the means of happiness for the world, and so he vows to serve this ideal with his knowledge. The long monologue in which this resolution is born begins with a homely metaphor: a grape, though a small fruit, needs a full summer and many, many rays of sunlight to mature, so the world, a much larger fruit, must need millions of years—but it, too, will eventually mature. The rays that nurture it, however, are great men's souls, and these are not born often. He is such a ray, he realizes, and so he must set to work:

> Mi célja a világnak?
> Boldogság! s erre eszköz? a szabadság!

Szabadságért kell küzdenem,
Mint küzdtek érte oly sokan,
És hogyha kell, elvérzenem,
Mint elvérzettek oly sokan!
Fogadjatok, ti szabadság-vitézek,
Fogadjatok szent sorotok közé
Zászlótokhoz hűséget esküszön. . . .

What is the goal of the world? / Happiness! And the means to this end? Liberty! / I must strive for Liberty, / As so many others have done, / And if I must, I'll bleed to death / As so many others have done! / Accept me, you heroes of Liberty / Accept me among your ranks: / I swear allegiance to your banner. . . . (chapter 9, p. 1012)

This dedication is first tested when Szilveszter refuses a lucrative post in a grand man's retinue to serve as a notary for an unimportant village. But, because he teaches the people his ideas of liberty, he is driven away. What is hardest to bear is that the very men he had sought to help now turn against him. The only friend who remains true is the lord's daughter: she follows him and chooses to share his life.

New disappointments, however, follow. The great work he had been working on is not accepted by any publisher, since it cannot get the censor's approval. Thus, in order to earn something and provide for his family, he takes a copyist's job. As the years pass, the family increases to four and his great work still remains without a patron. This, then, is the state of affairs on that dark night when the hero contemplates his future.

The section concludes with the same lines that had served to introduce it: the rising sun brings the promise of better times. Ironically, events become even darker. The lines, however, link the various sections stylistically and indicate quite clearly that these eleven chapters form a separate unit within the poem.

The morning fails to live up to its promise. The infant dies at its mother's breast and Szilveszter must bear one more burden. However, instead of violent grief and recriminations, the poem strikes a minor key. The mother's sorrow is expressed in a tender lullaby. Death brings no real separation, she asserts in her gentle words:

"Alszol, kicsiny
Kis magzatom;
Mit álmodol? . . .
Hisz még nem a föld
Ölében alszol,
Anyád ringat még,
Anyád ölel.–
Aludj, aludj,
Szép gyermekem. . . .

Do you sleep / My little child; / What do you dream? / . . . Not yet do you sleep / In the earth's bosom, / Your mother rocks you still, / Your mother hugs you; / Sleep, sleep, / My beautiful child. . . . (chapter 15, p. 1029)

Even when she contemplates the little grave, all the mother can think of is the time they will spend together as she speaks to the child. The effect of the whole scene is a relief from suffering: the dead child is almost envied by the others.

After this sentimental interlude, Szilveszter seems to be at last on the verge of success: an underground press publishes his work. But the moral victory he savors is brief: the authorities soon move against him. Before he is silenced, however, he delivers a denunciation of the "criminal king." He curses the king in words that evoke the violence of the French Revolution. Instead of support, however, he only gains hatred, even among the masses in whose name he speaks. He is most enraged, however by the lack of decency shown by man to man: he would go to prison meekly if only he were allowed to say farewell to his wife and child; he would consider his chains ornaments if only he would not be leaving behind him a helpless family. In prison, Szilveszter first rages against injustice, but with time he sinks into a stupor. The only thing that rouses him is a vision of his wife come to bid him farewell after her death. In a fit of anger, he seeks to commit suicide, but then settles into his old lethargy.

Ten years pass during which he loses all interest in life until one day a bird sings on the window of his cell. In a lyrical outburst, hope is reborn:

". . . Dalolj, dalolj, kis madaram, dalolj,
Eszembe jut dalodról,
Hogy egykor éltem, hogy még most is élek,
Eszembe jut dalodrul ifjuságom,
A régen régen elszállt ifjuság,
E szép tavasz, s ezen tavasznak
Virága, a szép szerelem!
Dalod fölkelti szenvedésimet,
De egyszersmind meg is vigasztal,
S a megvigasztalt fajdalom talán
Még édesebb, mint maga az öröm,
Dalolj, dalolj, kis madaram, dalolj!" . . .

"Sing, sing my little bird, sing / Your song reminds me / That once I lived, and even now am alive, / Your song brings back my youth, / The long, long ago lost vigor, / This lovely spring, and the spring's / Flower, beautiful love! / Your song rouses my griefs / But at the same time consoles them, / And pain consoled is perhaps / Even sweeter than joy itself, / Sing, sing my little bird, sing." (chapter 18, p. 1046)

Such alternation between scenes of deep despair, rage, and hopeless stupor with the images of hope and renewal was characteristic of Petőfi. Here, however, he used the technique more consistently and more skillfully than he had done in the briefer lyrics. The device adds to the success of the narrative: it provides the relief needed in any tragedy. Appropriately, into what seems the most hopeless period of Szilveszter's life, a promise of better things is introduced. Szilveszter believes that the bird, the free creature of free skies, is a messenger of hope and freedom, and he rallies. After all, he concludes, the world must grow weary of its chains and shame will eventually rebel. Fittingly, the bird does prove to be an omen, and Szilveszter is soon set free.

Upon his release, he seeks his old home, but no one there can tell him where his wife lies buried or what has become of his son. Worse still, the nation is not free, but has sunk even deeper into servitude. Yet, he still hopes:

Hiába volt hát annyi szenvedés,
Hiába annyi áldozat,

Mit a magasztosabb szivek hozának
Az emberiségnek? haszontalan
Minden törekvés, minden küszködés?
Az lehetetlen, százszor lehetetlen!

Was such suffering then in vain, / In vain such sacrifice / Which nobler hearts have brought / For mankind? Useless / All effort, all struggle? / That is impossible, a hundred times impossible! (chapter 19, p. 1051)

Out of desperation, he formulates a plan: he will kill the king, and thus eliminate the source of all oppression.

This final resolution taken, he mingles with the festive crowds that cheer the king, shouts, "Let the king die," and fires his weapon. The apostle of freedom, however, is reviled by the masses who gladly see him executed in a few days' time. Unsuccessful in his own time, Szilveszter regrets he had paid such a high price for human blindness that *will* not see.

In the concluding chapter, Petőfi presented the future: later generations, better than their fathers, do gain the freedom Szilveszter had sought, and glorify these martyrs of the cause.

Petőfi left the time and scene of this poem vague. While it is clear that the narrative is set in a time close to the poet's own, little else is specified. The relative modernity of the poem is seen in the liberal and revolutionary sentiments worked into the romantic tale, but more importantly in the emphasis on an urban setting, the constant mention of the press, and the threat of censorship. The locale, left similarly undetermined, could be any country where the evils Szilveszter combats were found: censorship, the privileges of birth and wealth, the oppression of new ideas.

However, the poem is not vague, and in the details that lend realism to the story it is clear that Petőfi is writing about a composite picture of the Austrian monarchy he seems to have evolved. This is based on the knowledge of poverty and hardship that he himself had faced in his wanderings, and his often unnecessary conflicts with authority of almost every kind. Quick to take offense himself, he was supersensitive to what he imagined to be the misuse and abuse of power. Thus, he exaggerated what he knew and created a poem against a personified Tyranny, not against oppression in any one country or at any one time. The theme of the poem is not one man's struggle against evil, but rather the search for an answer to the question of how this evil (tyranny, oppression, injustice) can be resisted. Is a futile fight worth the effort? Is it justified? Petőfi had to face these questions in the summer of 1848, but they are questions that had been valid earlier and have continued to be valid. Thus, the poem does touch on universal themes, and the vagueness of the setting is appropriate.

CHAPTER 7

The Last Year

I *Personal Lyrics Against the Background of War*

THE poems of the last period of Petőfi's life were almost exclusively concerned with public events. He urged the country to unite in the face of threats to its newly won independence and to defend the democratic principles of March 15. Some thirty poems are calls for rededication or reminders of duty. These were addressed to the country as a whole, to the legislators, to the poets, even to himself. Another eighteen are war poems: marches, battle songs, songs of praise and commemoration. There is a group of thirteen revolutionary and antiroyalist poems, many of them narratives taken from Hungarian history and used to illustrate abuses of royal power. Only twenty-four out of over ninety poems are not specifically on these political or patriotic subjects; half of these are love poems, and the other half personal lyrics. However, even these reflect the poet's intense involvement in public affairs.

The love poems of this period were products of the turbulent turn of events in Petőfi's own life. He was no longer courting Júlia, but neither could he celebrate their domestic happiness. His duties with the army—first as a recruiter, later as a regular soldier—brought the first separation since their marriage. The lonelinesss of these days was captured in "Úton vagyok, s nem vagy velem" ("I'm Traveling, and You Are not with Me"), "Hideg idő, hűs őszi éj" ("Cold Weather, a Cool Autumn Night") and the one that expresses his mood most clearly, "Hogy volna kedvem" ("How Could I Be Glad"). The mood of all of these poems is melancholic and sentimental: in these days, her memory is his moon, and it sheds only a dim light. The images of brightness earlier associated with Júlia are thus transformed.

The sad mood is clearly indicated by the many watery images and the frequent references to tears.

The war, however, also brought happier moments. On the way to Júlia's parents at Erdőd, they stopped at Nagykároly, the scene of their first meeting, and he captured those distant days in a few memorable lyrics. In "Tudod, midőn először ültünk" ("You Know, When First We Sat Here"), Petőfi admitted that the past two years had taken much from him, but they had also brought him much more in giving him "The bright pearl strand of his hopes." She makes up for any loss he might have suffered. As in most of these poems, however, separation is never far, so Petőfi concluded:

Maradjunk még itt, légy mellettem . . .
Hol úgy busúltam egykoron,
Hagyj engem itt most elmerengnem
Végtelen boldogságomon!

Let us stay; be beside me . . . / Where once I sorrowed so / Let me muse now / On my endless happiness. (1064)

In another poem[1] Petőfi addressed the trees under which he first saw his beloved. He compared the progress of their love to stages of the day, recalling its joyous dawn as he enjoys the warmth of its noon and looks forward to the twilight of his love many years in the future. Even when they are dead, Petőfi suggested, their love shall shine like a star over their "green graves / On dark-blue nights." Petőfi's lyrical poems continued to capture the mood of the moment in a brief image or in a telling line or phrase, as the adjective "dark blue" illustrates: it suggests a gentler night than "black" would, particularly since it is placed next to the "green" of the previous phrase. Colorful visual images continue to characterize Petőfi's poetry and show an even more skillful use than in earlier poems as a proof of his continuing lyrical mastery.

The most important love poems of this time were those in which he paid tribute to his wife as a worthy partner in the great work he was engaged in. "Feleségem és kardom ("My Wife and My Sword") is a playful dialogue between the poet and his sword. The weapon, presented as a gruff old taskmaster, seems to object to his dallying with a wife, but the poet points out that there is really no conflict: she loves him far too much to let him shirk his duty. Instead, she will tie the sword on his side and send them off together when the need comes. Petőfi established a light, bantering tone partly through the gradual description of the scene in the manner of the folksong:

Galamb van a házon,
Csillag van az égen,
Az én ölemben van
Kedves feleségem;

Ugy tartják szelíden
Ringató karjaim,
Mint a harmatot a
Rezgő fa lombjai.

Dove on the housetop, / Star in the sky, / My dear wife / Is in my arms; / My rocking arms / Hold her so gently, / Like the dew is held / By the tree's trembling foliage. (905–6)

But he also selects images that suggest the basically serious theme: the trembling dewdrop suggests the transience of this moment of happiness which they prefer to consider as timeless—just as the dewdrop is unaware of the brevity of its existence.

On a more serious note, but essentially the same subject, is "Három madár" ("Three Birds") in which Petőfi compares three qualities of his wife with his three favorite birds: her good humor is like the merry titmouse which sings the whole winter through; her heart is the nightingale whose song entrances all by its sweetness and sadness, but her soul is the eagle which flies into the face of storms, allowing himself to be carried away by it. The suggestion, of course, is that she will stand by him in his public life and not distress him with her laments. Sharing his ambitions, she was a partner in his life, not only a passive helper.

When both the battles and the political maneuverings were going badly, he turned to his wife for consolation. "Itt benn vagyok a férfikor nyarában" ("Here I Am in the Summer of Manhood") is a lament for all the grand plans that seem to have been lost. A series of nature images captures the desolation he feels, but each stanza ends with the consolation: "Milyen sötét vón a világ, az élet, / Ha nem szeretnél, fényes angyalom!" ("How dark the world and life would be, / If you did not love me, my bright angel!" 1055). To appreciate Petőfi's ability to evoke a mood through his images, it is necessary to trace these in the poem. The first stanza laments the spring that has carried with it the "many beautiful flowers" and "the melodious lark" of his dreams. The scene becomes even more somber in the next stanza: the red rays of the sun have fled the sky and the singing birds the earth, leaving only "sad breezes or angry storms" to sing in the empty nests. The sense of desolation extends to his reverie "in whose dry forests the foliage rattles." Since the promise of life and hope is gone from the sounds of nature, so, too, is its brightness: the "golden daystar of the sky" and the silver dew of the earth have been obscured and dried out by the dark clouds and dry heat of reality. He himself, who had often drunk of the "fairy stream of ambition," no longer thirsts for glory, and all that remains is their love for each other: in Julia he seeks light and warmth, the sun and the stars.

This elegy, in the tens pattern with three stresses per line and almost no pause within the lines, uses a fairly regular falling meter and a well-defined *a b a b c b c d* rhyme to emphasize the slow sounds, low vowels, and liquid consonants—all of which contribute to the subdued tone of the poem. The poet felt that all of his hopes for a better world must be abandoned; but the hurt, though personal, went beyond that. The reason he was not recognized as a great poet, Petőfi felt, was because the nation was not ready for the steps he advocated. In this universal darkness, he appealed to Júlia:

Szeress, szeress, mint én szeretlek téged,
Oly lángolón, oly véghetetlenűl,
Áraszd reám a fényt s a melegséget,
Mely isten arcáról szivedbe gyűl;
Az a te szíved egyetlen világom,
Nappal napom és éjjel csillagom . . .
Milyen sötet vón a világ, az élet,
Ha nem szeretnél, fényes csillagom!

Love me, love me, as I love you, / So burningly, so infinitely, / Shed on me the light and the heat / Which is gathered in your heart from God's face; / Your heart is my sole light: / My sun by day, my star at night. / How dark the world and life would be, / If you did not love me, my bright angel! (1056)

While intense and original, such a poem was not unique. The same kind of devotion was expressed in "Búcsú" ("Farewell"), written at the conclusion of a fleeting visit to his wife during the Transylvanian campaign. This poem illustrates the way in which Petőfi used his most personal lyrics to justify himself, to explain his actions, and to provide a model or inspiration for others. While this might seem egotistical, it is understandable if we recall Petőfi's almost religious dedication to poetry: he considered it a sacred calling, and to fail to use his talents for the education and inspiration of others would have seemed cowardly.

The poem makes two important statements: (1) he does not leave his wife in order to seek glory, but because his country needs him and he has an obligation to fulfill; and (2) should he return maimed from the battlefield, their love will remain as strong as ever. Such encouragement was meant for all men who had to leave their families, and while the elegiac mood prevails, it is modified by the assurance that love will endure. The metrics of the poem reflect this same blending of permanence and transience, particularly in the refrain that forms a third of each stanza and incorporates the formula of parting: "Isten veled, szép ifju hitvesem, / Szivem, szerelmem, lelkem, életem!" ("God be with you, my beautiful young wife; / My heart, my love, my soul, my life," 1067).

No conflict ever seems apparent between the certainty Petőfi felt in Júlia's support of all he did and her feelings. Though accused later of betraying his memory in a second marriage, Júlia was true to her husband during his lifetime, and seemed not to have complained of the loneliness and privations that his devotion to his own ideals and to the cause of the Revolution brought on her. His last lines to her, a brief letter written a few days before his death, showed concern, but no anxiety. He wrote that he had received a letter from Bem, whom he was seeking to join, and hoped to catch up with the general either in Brassó or beyond. He promised to write whenever he could, and urged her to be patient, concluding: "Believe! Hope! Love! Your husband faithful to the grave and even beyond, Sándor."[2] In spite of the reference to death, however, the poet was not seeking it. He and Júlia planned to settle in Transylvania among the Székelys after the war, and made plans quite cheerfully. There was a streak of melancholy in the poet, however, and he often joined the deepest thoughts of love with the idea of death, as if to emphasize the eternity of his love in contrast to the transience of life. In his poetry this joining of the two ideas, love and death, became expressions of a deep human truth. Few readers find it morbid there; yet in the letter, because the form is more literal,many have been misled. But Petőfi's prose cannot be separated from his poetry: both are expressions of his impetuous nature, and such a letter is no more studied than a lyrical outburst of emotion.

The other personal lyrics are on a variety of themes. Two celebrate his native region, somewhat in the manner of his earlier landscape poems; two commemorate important events in his life;[4] and three can be regarded as attempts to escape the public arena for a few quiet moments.[5] The other five, while neither war songs nor political poems, are still concerned with the war.

The two important personal events commemorated were the birth of his son and the death of his parents. In the former, while he rejoiced in the birth of the child, he saw in him someone who would continue his patriotic work. It is an expression of the same commitment that is found in the love poems. His joy in holding his son is not purely personal: he will raise little Zoltán to benefit the country, and not merely as his own. And, should he die in the coming battles, the "homeland will not suffer. / No, for his soul lives on in his son."

The lament for his parents, who died within months of each other while Petőfi was away,[6] was an unrestrained burst of grief at their grave. He felt he had been left completely alone, and the only consolation he could take with him was the sight of their headstones, extending a pair of arms in a seeming embrace. In this poem, the didactic quality, which is never quite absent from the other personal lyrics, seems lacking. There is no public stance, only private grief. As such, the poem is almost unique in Petőfi's work. The only comparable lyrics are a few "escape" poems.

In these, Petőfi's dedication to his conviction that he would make an impact on his country and on the world is not evident. They illustrate that there were times when he longed to retire from the constant fight this role brought with it. A day spent in the hills of Buda was captured in "A hegyek között" ("In the Mountains"): as he watched Júlia playing like a child among the flowers, he, too, was renewed. "Itt van az ősz, itt van ujra" ("It's Fall, It's Fall Again") allowed him to meditate on his favorite season, autumn, developing the parallels between sleep and the rest that this season signals for Nature. Written in the meter and style of the folksong, it struck an unusually gay tone, although in the final stanzas the tempo slows as he and his wife seem to sink into the harmony of the sleeping scene.

But the patriotic images and the call of duty were not absent for long. The memory of former happy days spent with Júlia was evoked in "Elpusztuló kert ott a vár alatt" ("Fading Garden by the Castle"), but in this he introduced images of lost national glory in the ruins of an ancient castle of the Rákóczis. The memories of his courtship in the garden seem to be in contrast to such a somber setting—but is it really? The sadness of the poem is distilled in the final stanza in which the poet wonders if there will ever be lovers again in the garden or admirers of the castle's heroes.

At times, Petőfi seems to have feared that his responsibilities as a citizen and a soldier might still his lyrical voice, or at least render inappropriate certain of his favorite themes. For example, "Miért kisérsz" ("Why Do You Attend Me?") expressed a cry of rebellion that he must forget his youth and his wife: "Tavasz, költészet, szerelem! / El hagyjam őket tőlem szállani?" ("Spring, poetry, love! / Shall I allow these all to fly away from me?" 923). Even his New Year's Eve poem in 1848 was a lament: he must put aside poetry now, and if he writes at all, he must write war poems. But in spite of this pessimism, Petőfi wrote three lyrics in that year which show that his fears were unfounded. His lyrical power was not diminished; it developed and showed even more mastery than before.

In "A tavaszhoz" ("To Spring") he appealed to this season

of renewal to heal the wounds of the war. The world had waited long for her healing power:

Ifju lánya a vén télnek,
Kedves kikelet,
Hol maradsz, mért nem jelensz meg
A világ felett?

Young daughter of ancient winter, / Dear Springtide, / Where do you tarry, why do you not come / To the world? (907)

But the poet assured the world that spring will come with her "sky-blue tent," the lark's song, and flowers by the handfuls to cover the graves of Liberty's heroes. It will prove that the realm of death, though growing ever larger, is not without hope.

A lull in the fighting seems to have inspired "Pacsírtaszót hallok megint" ("I Hear Again the Song of the Lark"). The harbinger of spring reminded him that he was not only a soldier ("an instrument of killing") but also a poet. The song's promise of new life awoke memory and hope, and those "twin rose bushes" bloomed again in his heart. Yet the images of war faded slowly. The healing was gradual, and the "dear little bird's" song was like a cool mountain stream upon a burning wound. It came after the noise of battle had ceased, and the gentler images slowly won out as the barrenness of his own heart was gradually replaced:

Dalolj, pacsirta, hangjaid
Kikeltik a virágokat:
Szivem mily puszta volt és benne már
Milyen sok szép virag fakad.

Sing, oh lark! your notes / Awaken the flowers: / How empty my heart was and / Already how many lovely flowers are budding in it. (1109)

A similar transformation is the subject of "Ki gondolná, ki mondaná" ("Who Would Think, Who Would Say"). Returning to a battlefield some weeks after the battle, he found no trace of the fight In a series of parallel images he presented the two scenes, using the basic dividend eights of the folksong in *a b c b* quatrains. The form already indicated that a lighter tone would balance the somber scenes of battle, and each quatrain emphasized this by being divided into the two contrasting scenes: then, the sky was sullen like a man's worries; now it was like a small child's eyes, gentle and clear blue; then the earth was white, like an old man's head; now it is green, like a young man's hope. The suggestion of death versus renewal, despair versus hope, is carried over into the next stanza in which the song of the lark was contrasted to the whistling of cannon balls. The limit of such parallelism is almost reached in the final stanza, where the poet alludes to the bodies of the dead which seem to have been replaced by flowers. Thus, though the events of 1848–1849 often forced Petőfi's more lyrical poetry to the background, he did not abandon it. The style and the concerns, or perhaps only the subjects and the emphasis changed, but the poet remained true to the vocation to which he had dedicated himself years earlier.

II *Revolutionary Poetry*

Petőfi, convinced that the future of Hungary lay in independence from Austria, wrote several poems urging a complete break with the Habsburg dynasty. He conjured up the spirit of Rákóczi[7] and warned against delays.[8] He attacked all kings, but particularly the Habsburgs who had never proved themselves friends of the nation. "A királyokhoz" ("To the Kings") was an early and relatively mild attack. Still, it drew criticism, such as the poems that concentrated on the renewal of Hungary and the restoration of its lost powers did not. The allegory, "A ledőlt szobor" ("The Fallen Statue") urges men to restore this fallen giant to its former beauty and to raise it again on a pedestal. "A két ország ölelkezése" ("The Embrace of the Two Countries") suggests that those who found him too militant did not realize that his poems were warnings and that even greater upheavals would follow unless the reforms were swift and substantial. He let the opportunists know that he saw through them in "A márciusi ifjak" ("The March Youths"): many have usurped this title who had hung back timidly in the days when the Revolution was being made. However, Petőfi goes on to declare that even such support is good as long as the cause and the country is served. The goal is to serve the nation, he asserts in "Miért zárjátok el az utamat?" ("Why Do You Block My Path?"). His desires draw him forward, but he only seeks to serve, not to gain fame.

The antimonarchial poems of this period can be divided into the narratives and the warnings. The former chronicle the abuses of royal prerogative; the latter give clearer and clearer notice to the Habsburgs, and to all kings, that they are anachronisms whose days are surely over. The extreme hatred seen in some of the later poems[9] is understandable as the result of the contemplation of past abuses and bitterness at the king's continued highhandedness. Most were written after the young king, Franz Joseph, reneged on the oath of his predecessor and even encouraged the invasion of the country by Jellačiś as well as rebellion by the nationalities. Involved as Petőfi was in both the promising beginnings of the Revolution and its ever more disastrous conclusion, he grew bitter, and this bitterness often took control of his poetry.

The narrative poems, mostly brief and quite explicit in their message, chronicle the weakness of Andrew II who allowed his foreign wife too much power ("Bánk Bán"); the treachery of Louis V in the execution of László Hunyadi ("A király esküje"; "The King's Oath"); and the execution of an early opponent of royal absolutism ("Kont és társai"; "Kont and His Companions"). Two others, "Dobzse László" and "Kun László krónikája" ("The Chronicle of László Kun") ridicule two of the more inept rulers of Hungary. Though some of these poems exhibit a lively style, especially the ballad on the tragic death of the elder of János Hunyadi's two sons, none are truly important. In fact, of this group only the jeremiad "Ausztria," and "Vérmező,"[10] the lament on all the bloodshed seen by the old castle of Buda, can be considered more than propaganda pieces.

The former draws a parallel between the destruction of Jerusalem and the destruction that will overtake Austria, leaving her rulers penniless beggars driven from land to land. The latter is a dignified ode dedicated to the memory of all who had died in Buda Castle and on the "Field of Blood." It is particularly dedicated to the memory of the five patriots who were executed for their parts in the Martinovics revolt. Petőfi could accurately cite the old abbot's defense that when the interests of the country and the king come into conflict, it is the king who must die. Since the tribute he felt was due these heroes could not be given at the time of their deaths, this ode honors them belatedly.

The poem unites often grisly images with those of gentle beauty. The opening stanza presents the old castle which

> Sok gyászdolgot látott, hosszú életeben,
> Sok gyászdolgot látott, megirtózott tőle,
> Azért várja, várja, hogy már mikor dől le?

[Buda castle] had seen many mournful things in its long life, / Seen many mournful things, and been repelled by them; / And so it waits, it awaits the time—when shall it tumble down? (967)

The headless ghosts of Buda and the thirsty field of blood evoke the horrors of the past, but the description of the day of the execution promises renewal, even if the decree cannot be altered: "Május hónapja volt, hajnal volt az égen, / Rózsa a kertekben, vér a vesztőhelyen" ("It was the month of May, dawn was in the sky, / Roses in the garden, blood on the gallows place," 969). This fairly formal ode is in the "divided twelves" or alexandrine favored for dignified poems; the slightly archaic effect is heightened by the couplet rhyme and the steady pace the narrative receives from the built-in stops within each stanza and verse. It is one of Petőfi's traditional poems, and shows his skill in using the romantic meters, moods and even vocabulary to advantage when the subject is suitable.

Though Petőfi's early poetry was patriotic, it was not particularly nationalistic. However, as the attacks on the newly autonomous country increased from both within and without, he not only praised the "Magyar," but began to criticize the other nationalities of Hungary. In addition to the Germans (by whom he generally meant the Austrians), he struck out against the Serbs and Rumanians, and even some of the national minorities. The Austrians, identified with the Habsburgs, drew disdain rather than rage, but Petőfi was angry at the others because he believed they were cowards and opportunists who served the interest of their own oppressors against the new Hungarian state which could give them freedom. The poems of these times were martial odes like "Élet vagy halál" ("Life or Death"), "Már minékünk ellenségünk" ("The Whole World is Our Foe"), and "Fekete-piros dal" ("Black and Red Song"), or biting satires that rejected any thought of compromise such as "Mit nem beszél a német" ("What the Germans Won't Say") and "Hány hét a világ" ("How Many Weeks is the World"). In proud poems like "Ismét magyar lett a magyar" ("The Magyar has become Magyar Again"), Petőfi urged that the tradition of independence for which his nation had been famous in the past be honored and preserved.

The odes to the nation, to liberty, and to the Székelys[11] emphasized the positive side of this nationalism. Thus, "A Székelyekhez" ("To the Székelys") is a call to this brother-nation, as he calls it, to join forces with the Magyars. They can count on no other allies, he declared, because the whole world is their enemy, and those who enslaved the one also conquered the other. They must be confident in their cause—"for truth and God is with us"—and must unite, he urges; only in this way will they win against Vienna and its allies. As was to be expected, his ode to liberty[12] was an equally confident statement that this long-neglected and persecuted godhead would finally receive the honors due her:

Te vagy a mi törvényes királyunk,
Trónusodnál ünnepelve állunk,
Körülötted miljom s miljom fáklya,
Meggyúlt szíveink lobogó lángja.

You are our legal king, / Celebrating, we stand round your throne, / Surrounding you, a million and a million torches, / The flame of our burning hearts. (892)

There is something Shelleyan in the poet's absolute assurance of the ultimate triumph of Good (Liberty) over Evil (Tyranny). This is true even in the poems written when things were not going well and when it looked as if Austria would triumph after all.

A free verse ode, "1848," suggests that the year will usher in a new age. In an effective reversal of the "ship of state" metaphor, Petőfi presents the "moving earth" and "dry waves" which will upset the boat and tumble the panic-stricken pilot from it, still "wrapped in his ragged purple." Looking forward to the free centuries that are to follow, he uses another daring image: the prophecy of the Scriptures has been fulfilled, as now there is truly only one flock and one shepherd in the one religion of Liberty. The imagery of the political poems of these months is full of such adaptations of the usual, even of the cliché. Petőfi repeated the same themes, the same ideas over and over, yet his attitude, voice, and mood changed constantly.

The grand future the poet saw in these poems could not, he knew, be won without sacrifice. That is why he wrote a series of poems urging action. A good example is "Mit daloltok még, ti jámbor költők? ("What Are You Still Singing, You Meek Poets?") in which he posed the rhetorical question: what good is the lark's song, if it is lost amid the thunderclaps? He quickly answered it: this is no excuse: the poet's song is needed now more than ever: Just as the lark does not care whether he is heard on earth but only sings for himself and for God, so they, too, must sing: "Let our songs fall onto / These cold ruins like the green ivy." Not only the inspiration of song is needed, but its consolation and promise as well.

Sentiments similar to these motivated his response to accusations of cowardice printed by Imre Vachot. His former employer had called him a braggart in the *Nemzetőr*: "Now, the war is on our necks; the country needs every able-bodied man; you had been a soldier, have no child, and yet your great sword, which you rattled so terribly in the March days, is still rusting in its scabbard."[13] Though the facts were not accurate—Petőfi had been a member of the Committee of Safety and also a Nemzetőr, or member of the national guard, almost as soon as it was established, and Júlia was expecting their first child in three months—Petőfi replied in the *Életképek* with "Hallod-e szív szívem?" ("Do You Hear Heart, My Heart?"). In it he showed himself to be upset not so much by the attacks of ignoble souls as by the power their words had to agitate him. He should be above such things, he told himself, and he would do his duty as he had always done it—but not because he sought the approval of such petty journalists.

Petőfi knew that he could serve his country with his pen better than with his sword, and even as a soldier the most valuable service he rendered was in inspiring the soldiers, in explaining the cause to them, and in serving as interpreter and liaison between General Bem, who knew not a word of Hungarian, and his soldiers, the Hungarians and Székelys who admired him but understood neither German nor French. Yet the reference to the "rusty sword"—his own words from the "National Ode"—must have stung. In any case, he had been considering enlistment, waiting chiefly because of Júlia's condition, but now joined within a few weeks.

The year 1849 proved to be a time of war. Much of what Petőfi wrote was inspired by his experiences in the army and his participation in the Transylvanian campaign under Bem. One of these, "Európa csendes, ujra csendes" ("Europe Is Quiet, Is Quiet Again"), shows the faith he had in the nation as he urged that the struggle be continued, even though Hungary has been left alone:

Európa csendes, ujra csendes,
Elzúgtak forradalmai . . .
Szégyen reá! Lecsendesűlt és
Szabadságát nem vívta ki.

Europe is quiet, is quiet again, / Its revolutions have subsided; / Shame on it! It has calmed down / And did not gain its freedom. (1101)

The promise of the movement that had swept Europe in the wake of the Paris revolution, and which almost reversed the conservative, absolute monarchies that had been reestablished by the Congress of Vienna a generation earlier, died. It was lost. Only in Hungary did the struggle continue. But, this is no cause for alarm, the poet says. Rather, let it be an inspiration:

Emelje ez föl lelkeinket,
Hogy mi vagyunk a lámpafény,
Mely amidőn a többi alszik,
Ég a sötétség éjjelén.

Let this raise our souls, / That we are the lamplight / Which, when the rest are asleep, / Burns in the night of darkness. (1102)

The final stanzas seek the blessing of Liberty on "Its only adherents / In this faithless age." The meter Petőfi used, alternating eight and nine syllable lines, with the corresponding four and three beats per line, gives the poem a dignified meter which, though slow, is quite forceful. The caesura after the second measure, the predominance of short, well-defined syllables, the confident ring of the words, all make it an anthem rather than a dirge.

The hopelessness of the last months, when Hungary had to face both Austria and Russia, formed the background to the poem, "Bizony mondom, hogy győz most a magyar" ("Truly I Say, Now the Hungarians Will Win"). Petőfi wrote a supremely confident poem because he felt that Right and Justice *must* triumph. The poem celebrates the unity of the nation that is finally "one soul, one heart, one arm." The moment of victory has to be at hand now that all personal jealousies and ambitions, all pettiness has been laid aside; the poet believes he himself will go into battle more confidently now:

> Mert én leszek, nekem kell lenni, ki
> Ha elleninket mind a föld fedi,
> Megéneklem majd diadalmadat,
> Szabadság, és a szent halottakat, . . .
> Meg kell, hogy érjem azt a szép napot,
> Midőn áldásodat reánk adod, . . .
> Meg kell, hogy érjem azt a nagy napot,
> Amelyért lantorm s kardom fáradott!

Because I know I will be, I must be he who, / When our enemies are all under the earth, / Will sing of your triumph / Liberty, and of the sacred dead, / . . . I must live to see that glorious day / When you give us your blessing, / . . . I must live to see that grand day / For which my lyre and my sword had labored. (1108)

Petőfi's confidence and trust in the ultimate victory of his cause was steadfast, but it was in the darker, more hopeless days of the war that he seemed most certain of an early victory. Like his hero Szilveszter, he believed that once men know what is right, they will all accept it and tyranny, which keeps its hold because men are ignorant, will fall. Even frequent disillusionment failed to shake his faith in the ultimate rightness of this view.

Of course, his own circumstances at this time favored such optimism. He knew he was useful and could see the results of his activity. Impatient with talk, with debates, with the built-in delays of the governmental machinery, he was now among soldiers and under a commander who seemed to be winning city after city. While the rest of the country was slowly lost, in Transylvania victory seemed close. Petőfi's love and admiration for Bem also contributed to his optimism. Thus, however briefly these sentiments dominated in his life, they contributed to the creation of the proud sentiments in his war poems.

III *War Poems*

Some of Petőfi's best poetry was directly inspired by the war that followed the invasion of the country by the Croatian armies of Jellačiś, who were openly supported by the Imperial government, in September of 1848. This is quite natural, for from his early years he had dreamt of great deeds and honor won on the battlefield. Appropriately, one of the first of the war poems was an anacreontic, the "Bordal" ("Wine Song"). In the tradition of this genre he urged all men to toast the homeland with a glass of wine in one hand, a sword in the other. When the days of battle come, they will win their freedom "draining blood and life" from anyone who seeks to destroy it "as we empty this glass." Petőfi used a traditional form, the divided eights with its four-four pattern—with the stress on the first measure of each half line—so that the poem has a well-defined beat that is enhanced by the end-stopped lines and couplet rhyme.

The bravery he urged here was amply demonstrated in the war. Regiments of Hungarian soldiers stationed abroad returned to defend their home. The march of one such group from the frontiers of Galicia is commemorated in "Lenkei százada" ("Lenkei's Squadron"). The ballad relates how this hussar regiment had heard the news of the Revolution and left their posts. When the commander heard of their desertion, he sought the cause and, learning it, unhesitatingly joined them. Petőfi took this contemporary and not uncontroversial incident and turned it into a spirited poem of praise. Significantly, he placed the emphasis on the soldiers themselves, not the commander, who is praised chiefly in terms of his rapport with the soldiers and for his willingness to join them in their return to Hungary.

But it was not only the trained soldiers who joined the defensive forces, and Petőfi was particularly sensitive to the contributions of the others. "A vén zászlótartó" ("The Ancient Standard-Bearer") commemorates his own father's participation in the rout inflicted on Jellačiś when the Croatian *bán* first ventured into Hungary in the summer of 1848. Old and ill, he still joined the young men, and Petőfi used this incident to praise all men who responded to the call of the homeland.

Nor was he unaware of the sacrifices the civilians made. The ballad "Péter bátya" ("Uncle Peter") shows the pride of an old man whose three sons have just enlisted. Peter even chides his wife for weeping when she should rejoice that they have sons to give for the country.

Though Petőfi was an officer, he always felt uncomfortable with the prerogatives of rank. In his opinion, more recognition should have been given to the common soldier who bore the brunt of the fighting. These thoughts are expressed in "Tiszteljétek a kőzkatonát" ("Respect the Foot-Soldier"). What seemed particularly ironic to him was that these men often had a vague idea at best of the principles for which they fought, received little in the way of benefits, and could not be assured of rewards after the war. Yet they fought bravely.

During the Transylvanian campaign and as a member of the national army, Petőfi came to know these men even better. He was particularly impressed by the bravery of the Székely soldiers, and in a short ode paid tribute to them. In his letters he had referred to the gaiety and determination of these men in battle,[14] and it is these qualities that he singles out in "A székelyek" ("The Székelys"). He does not have to lead them into battle with the command, "forward," he declares in the poem; they go into the thick of the fighting anyway, singing, with flowers in their hats as if going to a wedding:

Ki merne nékik ellenállani?
Ily bátorságot szívében ki hord?
Mennek, röpűlnek, mint a szél, s űzik
Az ellenséget, mint a szél a port!
Csak nem fajult el még a székely vér,
Minden kis cseppje drágagyöngyöt ér!

Who would dare resist them? / Who carries such bravery in his heart? / They go, they fly like the wind, and they drive / Before them the enemy like the wind the dust! / The Székely blood has not declined, / Each little drop is worth a precious gem. (1117)

The last two lines, with the emphasis gained by the rhyming of *vér* ("blood") and *ér* ("is worth"), are repeated at the end of each of the three stanzas, and so form a solemn declaration of the worth of these fighters.

The "Hovéds" or home guard, the volunteers who comprised the bulk of the forces, also drew Petőfi's praise. "A honvéd" was written in the form of an oath taken by the soldier to live up to this most sacred of all names next to God's and to defend the country faithfully. References to the justly deserved defeat of those who had "exploited this land . . . for three hundred years" are included, but so are expressions of joy at what was achieved by these dedicated men. The other side of a soldier's life is not ignored either. The speaker, who can easily and quite accurately be identified with Petőfi, longs for a reunion with his loved ones, even as he chooses death on the battlefield:

Társaim arcáról, akik elhullanak,
Én arról azt látom:
A hazáért halni legnagyobb boldogság
Ezen a vilagon!

From the faces of my fallen companions / I can see / That to die for one's homeland is the greatest joy / On this earth. (1123)

The appropriateness of these sentiments in view of Petőfi's own death makes the poem poignant, yet there is nothing sentimental or melancholy in the verses.

Petőfi's commander, General Bem, has often been mentioned. In view of his devotion and admiration for the Polish patriot who came to help the Hungarian cause when that of his own country was lost, it is not surprising that Petőfi wrote several poems about Bem. "Az erdélyi hadsereg" ("The Transylvanian Army") is a triumphant song promising victory:

> Mi ne győznénk? hisz Bem a vézerünk,
> A szabadság régi bajnoka!
> Bosszúálló fénnyel jár előttünk
> Osztrolenka véres csillaga.

Not win? Why, Bem is our leader, / The old champion of liberty! / He goes before us with a vengeful light / Osztrolenka's bloody star. (1112)

Between February 4 and 8, 1849, in a four-day campaign of retreats and consolidation in the face of forces that outnumbered them ten to one, Bem brought his troops into a position that enabled him to join the reinforcements from Hungary and thus take the city of Szeben. Petőfi, who wrote an account of this in his dispatches,[15] also commemorated it in a poem, "Négy nap dörgött az ágyú" ("Four Days the Cannon Roared"). In short, direct lines (alternating sevens and sixes) he sketched the bitter fighting that soaked with blood every inch of ground from Vízakna to Déva and reddened the newly fallen snow. The soldiers knew that victory was impossible and only fought for honor, but acquitted themselves well nevertheless. And such success as they had, he said, was due to "Bem, my heroic leader / My glorious general," whose own actions so inspired the army that it did not fall apart when newer and newer forces confronted them at each turn. Fully half the poem is an expression of his devotion to this general who was his friend and patron, and who once called him "mon fils," a compliment Petőfi considered the greatest he had ever received.

In "Vajdahunyadon" ("At Vajdahunyad"), a meditative poem about the ancient castle of the Hunyadis, Petőfi suggested that Bem must be a reincarnation of the fifteenth-century hero of the Battle of Belgrade. He had gone there with Bem, wishing to show off some of the important sights to this man whom he admired so much. Thus, the poem reflects this visit. In the partially descriptive first half, Petőfi recalled the great man who had lived there and who had shaken the "proud crescent on the towers of Constantinople." In the second half, it is the castle that speaks, incredulous that its ancient master has finally returned. Petőfi turns the poem into a novel dialogue between the ancient castle and the humble guest. In this way, the compliments to Bem could be delivered indirectly. Petőfi, the poet, could say what would have seemed sychopanthic in Petőfi the friend and subordinate.

Mindful of the need to communicate his enthusiasm and commitment to the soldiers on whom the conduct of the war depended, Petőfi wrote several battle songs or marches. "Csatadal" ("Battle Song") was written specifically for the troops, and Petőfi requested that twenty-five thousand copies be printed and distributed among them.[16] It verbalized the soldiers' intense feelings in a style that seemed to embody the action itself. The rhythm evoked the martial sounds mentioned in the first stanza, and the refrain moved the poem relentlessly forward:

> Trombita harsog, dob pereg
> Kész a csatára a sereg.
> Előre!
> Sűvit a golyó, cseng a kard,
> Ez lelkesíti a magyart.
> Előre!

Trumpets blare, drums beat, / Ready for battle stand the troops. / Forward! / Bullets whistle, swords clang, / This inspires the Magyar. / Forward! (1082)

The task of the soldiers is outlined in the following stanzas: the banner of Liberty must be held high for all the world to see; the Hungarians, who are all heroes, will face the enemy because their will and God's is one; if one should die, another will take his place; finally, even if all have to die, that is far better than if the country were lost. Soon, the lines were sung all along the front, and Petőfi noted with gratification yet another contribution to the war effort. He was particularly pleased that through such poems the simpler soldiers could understand what they were fighting for and would not die ignorant of the cause for which they lost their lives.[17]

Not all of the songs were so lofty. Aware of the needs of the people, Petőfi gave them light "verbunkós" songs also. These poems were reminiscent of the spirited recruiting ("Werbung") dances that had developed in the previous century. The "Bordal" already cited was a variation. "Van-e mostan olyan legény" ("Is There Such a Lad Now"), "Föl" ("Up"), and "Milyen lárma milyen vigadalom" ("What Noise, What Rejoicing") were others. Each of these poems is in a different form, yet each gives the same message: there is no one who will hang back now unless he is a coward. The first is the most spirited in both form and content. The setting is the battlefield, and both the imagery and the descriptive passages suggest the carnage: the thunderbolt at the speaker's head; the line upon line of fallen; the redness of the freely flowing blood. The pace of the poem is quick yet playful, because Petőfi used a half line after each line, giving an essential piece of information in this "tag" or else lightening the line by a humorous tangent:

> Van-e mostan olyan legény,
> Aki fél, . . .
> Bújjék bele a kemence
> Lyukába!

Is there now such a lad / Who's afraid?/ . . . Let him hide in the oven– / The brick oven! (898)

The half line, with two definite beats within three syllables, adds to the light and even humorous effect by the definite emphasis certain words thus receive. The next poem, "Föl," uses the familiar quatrain of alternating nines and eights. It has a less obvious, a less martial beat because, rather than a recruiting song, it is a preliminary encouragement to the village boys. It recounts the abuses and evils that need correcting and urges action. The last poem recreates carefree celebration in the tavern before the soldiers depart for the front.

Such lighthearted songs have a place in all war poetry and look back on a long tradition in Hungarian literature. But in the last months of the war, when both the gravity of the situation and what he considered the sacredness of the cause occupied his thoughts, Petőfi turned to more serious poems. "Föl a szent háborúra" ("Rise for the Holy War") called for a grand effort against the Russians. The form is similar to that of "Van-e mostan olyan legény?" in its use of half lines, but both the syllabic and metrical pattern is more complicated. Instead of merely alternating, the half lines here are used as the second and sixth lines and form a unit with the previous line. Also, the three syllables usually receive only one (variable) accent. This quicker line thus draws attention to itself by its departure from the regular (divided eights) beat of the rest of the poem rather than by the content. The effect of this complicated variation is a more dignified stanza and one that allows fuller development of each idea yet which is musically still linked to the marches. Also, as he had done in other poems, Petőfi used the last two lines in each stanza to comment on the situation he presented in the other six, setting them off by having them follow the half line, yet linking them by picking up the rhyme of that short line. For example, in the first stanza, he stated that the "last judgment" has arrived with the coming of the Russian forces, but in the last couplet he proudly says that this does not frighten him, either for himself or for his country. In the next stanza, he urged the defenders not to give up even against these great odds. In the final stanza, the possibilities of the form are again exploited. The opening line and half line contain the invocation "És te isten, magyarok nagy / Istene," which is followed by the request:

Légy népeddel, hű népeddel,
Jó népeddel, légy vele!

Tedd hatalmad fiaidnak
Lelkére,
Világdöntő haragodat
Fegyvereink élére!

And you, Oh God, great God of the / Magyars,[18] / Be with your people, your faithful people, / Your good people, be with them! / Lend your power to the spirits / Of your sons, / Your world-shaking anger / To the points of our weapons! (1125–26)

The religious fervor evident in this poem became more and

more pronounced in the last months of his life. Petőfi seemed to become even more dedicated to Liberty. In sincere poems he often called on God, who to him was the champion of the people against all oppressors. Petőfi's God became more and more identified with a powerful warrior fighting on the side of Right. Therefore, this is more than a call to arms; it is a summons to every man to stand up for "Freedom, God, and Country," against a wholly unlawful force (the king) who has brought in the "wild Cossacks" when his own forces could not win. The suggestion of a cosmic war between Good and Evil is intentional.

In this and other poems Petőfi referred to the "God of the Magyars," often identified with the Christian God but still claimed somehow uniquely for Hungary. "A magyarok Istene" ("The God of the Magyars") was also written to this power. The poet was confident that the God who had protected Hungary for a thousand years would not allow it to be lost when it was so close to reaching its goal of a better future. This poem, with its slightly archaic language and frequent scriptural imagery, sounds almost like a psalm. In it, Petőfi chided those who doubted the existence of this special Hungarian Providence, reassuring them in these words:

> Él az a magyarok istene, hazánkat
> Átölelve tartja atyai keze;
> Midőn minket annyi ellenséges század
> Ostromolt vak dühhel; ő védelmeze.

That God of the Magyars lives, our home / He enfolds in his fatherly hands; / When so many hostile centuries/ Besieged us with wild rage: He protected us. (908)

He reminded men that they would have been "like specks of dust blown before the wind" if his "sacred robe" had not been extended. In one of the startling nature images that make his poems memorable, Petőfi compared the mark of Divine Providence in Hungary's history with the face of the sun as it spans a river like a golden bridge. In this image Petőfi captured the contrast of earth and heaven, of the ever-changing and the eternal, and created a picture of human endeavor united, illuminated, enriched by divine guidance. At the same time, he suggested the new age that must come now when past sins, expiated in the centuries of strife, will be forgotten and virtues finally rewarded.

This confidence in the ultimate triumph of his cause, if not on the battlefield or the treaty rooms then at least in the judgment of history, can be sensed in one of the last battle songs Petőfi wrote. "Csatában" ("In Battle") is also notable for the personal involvement of the poet. By this time he had been in several battles, so he began the poem by recreating one such engagement:

A földön is harag,
Az égen is harag!
Kifolyt piros vér és
Piros napsugarak!
A lemenő nap oly
Vad bíborban ragyog!
Előre, katonák,
Előre, magyarok!

Wrath on the earth, / Wrath in the sky! / The red of spilt blood and/ The red rays of the sun!/ The setting sun glows/ In such a wild purple!/ Forward, soldiers,/ Forward, Magyars! (1106)

The next stanza also presented a double scene: the sun gazes in wonder from behind stern clouds; frightful bayonets glint in the smoke that wreathes darkly. Using onomatopoeic words, he gives an idea of the din of this battle in the next stanza: the long reports of the muskets, the earthshaking roar of the cannon must bring down heaven and earth. In the fourth stanza the poet steps back from the scene to show its effect on him: fired by enthusiasm, drunk with blood and fire, he rushes forward with the cry: "Utánam, katonák, / Utánam, magyarok!" ("Follow me, soldiers, / Follow me, Magyars! 1107).

This discussion of Petőfi's poetry concludes, appropriately, with his martial poems. Though a writer of beautiful love poems and romantic tales as well as a political, patriotic, and martial poet, he died shortly after writing this spirited and confident song. Furthermore, he died on the battlefield, at the conclusion of a day of intense and desperate fighting. But he lived on in legend and in his poetry. The legend is no longer of interest, but the influence he exerted on Hungarian literature cannot be ignored. Nor can the effect he had abroad, though short-lived and often based on the legend rather than the man, be dismissed.

CHAPTER 8

Petofi Abroad

I *Well-known yet Unknown*

OF all Hungarian poets, Petőfi is probably the best-known abroad. His poems have been translated into almost every written language. Encyclopedias and handbooks of literature mention him even if no other Hungarian figure is included. One or another of his poems generally has been included in the various anthologies of world literature so popular in the past century and the early decades of this one. He is probably the first Hungarian author of modern times to be known abroad during his lifetime. In view of the initial and even continued enthusiasm for the poet, it is surprising that his work as a whole and his actual literary achievements are little known. Few foreign readers have penetrated below the surface popularity.

The explanation for such broad and yet limited recognition lies in the myth that often surrounded Petőfi—especially after his death. He was regarded, especially abroad, as an unschooled, "natural" genius who represented the romantic and romanticized Hungarian "puszta." After the failure of the Revolution, he became to many a martyr and a hero who happened to write effective verses. The assessment of the poet's literary value suffered consequently, especially in the popular press in Hungary (once censorship was lifted in the late 1850s) and abroad. Thus, Bettina von Arnim put a Pindaric ode on Petőfi's lips ("Petőfi dem Sonnengott")[1] and made him a character in her rhapsodic work, *Gespräche mit Dämonen.* Hermann Grimm praised him as "the greatest poet of all peoples," and Carlyle considered him to be of equal stature with Goethe.[2] Yet none of these poets read him in the original, and they all knew him only through a very limited selection of his poems in the often inaccurate translation of Karl Maria Kertbény or Adolf Dux.

Even Heinrich Heine, whose own "Im Oktober 1849" is a poetic tribute to the Hungarians' tenacity in their fight for freedom and to Petőfi, had only a vague idea of the poet's true oeuvre.

II *A. Dux and K. M. Kertbény*

As might be expected, the German-language press in Hungary was the first to notice Petőfi. After 1844, critiques and comments on his work appeared with increasing frequency in the *Ungar*, the *Spiegel*, the *Pesther Tageblatt*, and other journals. Much of this reaction was both unfavorable and misinformed. For example, in March, 1845, L. Regnez reviewed *János Vitéz* in terms of a cynical fairy tale.[3]

By the end of 1846, however, these journals had translated nineteen poems,[4] and thus Petőfi broke through the language barrier and was soon known in Vienna and other parts of the German-speaking world. Adolf Dux, one of the early translators and critics, did much to make him known abroad; he acknowledged the young poet's popularity, but echoed many Hungarian critics in objecting to the "coarseness" of his poems. As is to be expected from journals concerned with transmitting an idea of the literary life of Hungary to its German-speaking inhabitants, each new work of Petőfi's was discussed, often with excerpts in German. Some of these translations, for example, C. Hoffman's in the *Pester Zeitung*,[5] were successful; others were not.

Adolf Dux was probably the first translator of Petőfi, for already in 1845 he had published three poems in the *Wiener Sonntagsblätter*. With *Ausgewählte Gedichte von Alexander Petőfi* (1846) he became the first among the translators to devote a separate volume to one poet. On the basis of this book he became accepted in Germany as the authority on Petőfi, a position Karl Maria Kertbény usurped only partially in the following decade. Not as voluminous a writer as Kertbény, Dux only published one other work on Hungarian literature: *Ungarische Dichtungen* (1854). In this, too, he included many of Petőfi's poems. In these two endeavors Dux strove to do more than merely make Petőfi's poetry available in German: he attempted to place Petőfi in the mainstream of European literature. He discussed the poet and his poetry in his prefaces and contributed much to the evolution of the "Petőfi myth." He also helped to make him a symbol of Hungary and the Hungarian Revolution.

In 1846, when the first volume of translations appeared, the reaction to Petőfi in Germany was varied. Dux had attempted to prevent misunderstandings by offering a detailed account of Petőfi's style and intentions, but the prevalance of misconceptions and ignorance about Hungary made difficult the appreciation of a poet who drew so fundamentally on the spirit of the nation for inspiration and on the life of his countrymen for imagery.

The German public considered Petőfi either a typical Hungarian peasant or a typical revolutionary, both of which assumptions were false. He was a unique man and did not fit completely into any category. Unfortunately, to augment the already difficult task of interpreting a poet of one nation to another nation, Dux lacked poetic talent and even failed to reflect the moods of his subject in his translations. Moreover, his critical insight was limited: he considered Petőfi simply as a folk poet, ignoring the richness of his literary heritage.

The second, and even more important, propagandist of Petőfi was Karl Maria Kertbény. Besides acquainting Heinrich Heine, Bettina von Arnim, and many lesser poets and translators with the poet, he carried Petőfi's fame beyond Germany. He corresponded with French and English literary men, and in England found an eager collaborator in the diplomat and linguist, Sir John Bowring, who helped promote Petőfi's fame in England and America.

Kertbény met Petőfi for the first time in 1846, when the latter was the much admired prodigy of Hungarian literature. The poet impressed the young critic very powerfully, and his short but brilliant career only heightened Kertbény's reverence for the poet. The tone of hero-worship never disappeared from his writing about Petőfi and, as a consequence, his critical evaluations often suffered. In this he was not unlike Dux; in fact, Kertbény carried his adulation to even greater length, especially in building up the Petőfi myth.

In 1847, one year after his first meeting with Petőfi, Kertbény published an account of the interview in the *Magazin für die Literatur des Auslandes* (1847) and laid the foundation for all the later representations of Petőfi as a wild-eyed enthusiast and "natural" poet who wrote by some sort of Delphic inspiration rather than by any discipline of poetic art. In the following years he published volume after volume on Petőfi and Hungarian literature. *Gedichte von Alexander Petőfi: nebst einem Anhang Lieder anderer ungarischen Dichter* appeared in 1849. It was followed by *Held János* (1850) and *Ausgewählte Ungarische Volkslieder* (1851). The last volume included some of Petőfi's folksong imitations. In 1852 Kertbény published his translation of Petőfi's novel under the title *Der Strick des Henkers.* Although most of the poems were from the early works of Petőfi and did not include his best political poems or his most mature genre pictures, they were enthusiastically received. *Held János* suffered in the translation, and it was never really appreciated abroad. On the other hand, Petőfi's novel did not deserve the popularity it received in Germany where its revolutionary tone appealed to the liberal faction. Encouraged by the reception of these early efforts, and helped by the suggestions of several German poets, Kertbény devoted his life to popularizing Petőfi and Hungarian literature abroad.

III *Petőfi in Germany*

Kertbény's methods, and the effect of his propagandizing, might be illustrated with reference to two German writers who responded to Petőfi more than most: Bettina von Arnim and Heinrich Heine. At the same time, this examination may help explain why, in spite of the great and genuine interest in Petőfi, he failed to exert a more enduring influence.

Heine's association with Hungary at first did not exceed the limits of the vague romantic admiration for an exotic land. In 1849, however, he met Karl Maria Kertbény in Paris, and in August of the same year he received a collection of Petőfi translations from the Hungarian critic. He was interested in these poems and wrote a few words about his reaction to Petőfi in a letter to Kertbény in September:

> You made me very happy with your book . . . Petőfi is a Poet who can only be compared to Burns and Béranger . . . so surprisingly healthy and primitive amid a society full of morbid and reflective ways, that I can place nothing beside him in Germany; I myself have only a few such natural sounds; on the other hand, his spirit seems to me not very deep, and all Hamlet-impulses are wholly absent from him, to his and his nation's fortune.[6]

It seems that he continued to read the poems sent him by Kertbény, for in October of the same year he wrote a poem which begins as an echo of Petőfi's "Europa csendes" and continues as a sort of comment or answer to it. I believe that the Petőfi poem, though not essential to the understanding of Heine's "Im Oktober 1849," nevertheless aids in its appreciation.

The first stanza, in particular, echoes the opening lines of Petőfi's poem:

> The strong wind has subsided,
> And it's quiet again at home;
> Germania, the great child,
> Again amuses itself with its Christmastrees.

Then, Heine refers to Ferenc Liszt who, unlike Petőfi, was still alive ". . . he does not lie, blood-red, /On a Hungarian battlefield; / Neither Russian nor Croat has murdered him." In the following verses he praises Hungary's defense of the cause of freedom and scorns Liszt for not sharing the common fate of his countrymen. He concludes with a typically romantic statement: the fate of Hungary was still better than that of Germany, for the former succumbed to the superiority of brute force, but the latter fell prey to intrigues and petty conquerors.[7] Petőfi's "Véres napokról álmodom" ("I Dream of Bloody Days") might have been another poem in Heine's mind when writing his tribute to the Hungarian heroes. This, too, had been included in the translations given him by Kertbény, and the battle imagery, or more precisely, the sound images suggested by battles —"Trompetenklange" ("Trumpet-sounds"), "das eisern wilde Kampfenlied" ("the wild iron battle song")—seem to echo the suggestions in Petőfi's poem. Perhaps the idea of a magnificent destruction, indicated by Heine's reference to the "Untergang der Nibelungen," was also suggested by the poem of Petőfi, although the theme was close enough to admit a parallel treatment without direct influence.

With Bettina von Arnim the impact of Petőfi was purely emotional. She considered him a kindred spirit and adopted him as a symbol of the ideals of the revolutionary movements of 1848. *Gespräche mit Dämonen* (1852), a loosely connected novel of dialogues about the rights of the people in which a young king is instructed in democratic ideas, reflects the background of the Hungarian Revolution. Bettina made use of the vivid accounts Karl Maria Kertbény had sent her of the last days of the war and expressed through this work the tribute of the liberal Germans. The Hungarians appeared early in the vision of the king in which his good spirit shows the victory of liberty over tyranny. The vision opened with a muster of the spirits of those who had fallen in the struggle for freedom, and the "Dämon" ("Genius") explained it to the sleeping king: "There, in the East, in the dusk the Swans wait together on the bank in the softly rising evening breeze, so that they can celebrate their farewell from the green banks of the homeland rivers with the rustling of wings. '*Eljen a haza!*'[8] rose the sounding rustle, so that the air echoed it and the roar of the sea was surpassed."[9]

Later in the vision the "Dämon" introduced Petőfi as a young soldier who had been killed in battle, but also as a poet, indicated by his shepherd's garb. He sang a lament addressed to the king who was now ready to make amends for his earlier tyranny. He reminded the ruler of the misery and destruction caused among his people in his name. He referred to the events in Hungary, mentioning the broken word of the monarch and General Haynau, who was the military governor of Hungary during the reign of terror that followed the surrender at Világos. Later, the "Magyargeister" ("Spirits of the Hungarians") are introduced, and the author suggests that Petőfi and his people should be taken as models by the Germans.[10] Bettina's correspondence with Kertbény between October 4, 1849, and December, 1850, made it clear that she considered Petőfi a genius, but also that she wholly misunderstood his style, if not his message.[11] Her *Gespräche*, like the apotheosis of Petőfi in the

"Sonnengott" poem, are highly subjective reworkings of his themes. Her suggestions on the translations Kertbény occasionally sent for comments further indicate that she could recognize Petőfi only as a lyrical poet, and one, moreover, who shared her rhapsodic tastes. She refused to accept any aspect of his poems that failed to conform to this view, and so sought to change *János Vitéz,* the poem Kertbény had selected to introduce Petőfi and Hungary to his German public, from the folktale that it was into an allegorical romance.[12]

Another prominent figure who was drawn to Petőfi's lyrics was Friedrich Nietzsche. As a young man he set to music four of Petőfi's early songs from the melancholy *Felhők.*[13] He also seems to have been attracted to the romantic image of Hungary as a child for, according to his sister, he wrote a piano fantasy entitled "Im Modschein auf der Puszta" at fourteen and a suite, "Ungarische Skizzen," a few years later. Other composers, too, found Petőfi's lyrics suitable for their music, notably the popular C. F. Daumer, who used some fifty-one poems, and who adopted some for his "Lieder."[14]

Though Dux and Kertbény were the first translators of Petőfi in Germany, they were soon followed by others. Before 1900, over thirty collections were published in Germany, Austria, and Hungary.[15] In many cases, these became intermediaries for the French, Italian, English, and Scandinavian versions. Moreover, the activity continued, if at a more moderate pace, into the twentieth century. The most recent edition of Petőfi's poems by Geza Engl, with translations by Martin Remane,[16] is possibly the best translation to date into a Western European language.

IV *The English Translations*

Petőfi's fame in England and America in some ways rivaled his popularity in Germany. Here, too, a translation appeared during the poet's lifetime, and here, too, the flow of exiles after 1849 helped spread his fame. In America the interest continued until World War I. Quite naturally, Petőfi was one of the first poets to benefit from the revival of interest in Hungary in the 1930s and the 1960s.

Sir John Bowring is the central figure in the introduction of

Petőfi's poetry to English readers. He had met Kertbény in 1847, and begun an extensive correspondence covering several years.[17] That same year he published two Petőfi poems in *Howitt's Journal.* Though the poems were inaccurate—no amount of poetic license can justify the complete change of content and mood found in these English versions—this did mean that Petőfi appeared in English within a year of the first translations of his poetry into German.

Since he knew no Hungarian, Bowring had to rely on Kertbény's German versions or the interpretation of the Hungarian emigrés with whom he established contacts after 1850. The effects of this wider and more critical group can be seen in Bowring's later works, particularly his 1886 volume, *Translations from Alexander Petőfi the Magyar Poet.* However, he was a man of mediocre talent, totally unaware of Hungarian literary traditions and the imaginative, emotional, or even actual world of Petőfi, and so his translations failed to give an accurate picture of the original.

But Bowring did contribute significantly to the recognition of Petőfi in England. The introduction to the *Translations* attempted to evaluate Petőfi for his English readers. He likened him to Robert Burns, a comparison that is only partially accurate, and he cited various German and French writers' views on the Hungarian poet. Thus, Bettina von Arnim's assessment of him as "the most original lyric poet in the whole world's literature," Alexander Humboldt's comment that "after many wanderings, he had discovered a flower so rich in beauty, so enduring, so certain to be valued," and the declaration by Hermann Grimm, professor of literature at Berlin, that Petőfi will rank among the very greatest poets of all times and tongues, are given.[18] He also cited the many translations of Petőfi's poems, both individual ones and collected works, in several European languages.

In the 1850s and 1860s and sporadically after that, Petőfi's popularity remained high in both England and America. Several translations appeared—as independent volumes or within anthologies.[19] The double limitations of the lack of an adequate command of Hungarian and mediocre talent persisted; even the first important American translator, William Loew, did not escape the latter.[20] The recent translations, such as *Sixty Poems by Alexander Petőfi*[21] issued on the centenary of the poet's death, and those included in the anthologies of Watson Kirkconnell or Joseph Grosz and W. Arthur Boggs,[22] contain some effective poems. They also show the continuing popularity of this poet who challenges translators again and again. The most recent effort in English worth mentioning is Victor Clement's *The Apostle* (1961).

There is again renewed interest, sparked by the one hundred and fiftieth anniversary of Petőfi's birth (1973). No acceptable English versions have been published so far, but his fame abroad has again been reassessed: by now, some of his poems have been translated into every major language. Altogether, they have appeared in fifty languages ranging from Albanian to Vietnamese and in thirty-six of these as independent volumes. The Czech, Danish, Finnish, French, Polish, German, Italian, Rumanian, Swedish, Serbian, and Slovak translations run into several volumes, with some dating to the 1850s and 1860s. Others—Arab, Estonian, Ukrainian—are more recent.[23] Petőfi is truly a poet of world literature who is known—well or slightly, truthfully or not—in every country of the world. That he is often known merely as a writer of folksongs, or as a revolutionary poet, a "poet of the people," is perhaps the result of his personality: the ideas come through even when the poetry is lost. This need not be a disadvantage; it should be a stepping-stone to the deeper appreciation of the poet.

CHAPTER 9

Conclusion

PETŐFI's contributions to Hungarian literature were quickly recognized. The first serious study was written by Pál Gyulai in 1854.[1] In it, the critic pointed out that Petőfi was not merely a writer of folksongs but a poet of great lyrical talent. He argued that Petőfi's poetry was great because, like all truly great works, it was based on "life, the poet himself, and the great creators of world literature."[2] He was not a philosophical poet; in fact, his philosophical poems are his weakest. But Petőfi could write about life as he saw it and as he experienced it, and he could make the individual experience ring true. This truthfulness gives his poems a universality even when they are intensely personal or most closely connected with Hungary. Thus, the love poem, "Reszket a bokor," has been translated some fifty times, and the patriotic poems made him equally popular in Germany, Italy, and Poland.

His familiarity with the great minds of world literature is proved by his extensive reading and especially his translations of Shakespeare (whom he considered the greatest of geniuses), Percy Bysshe Shelley, and Heinrich Heine. Nor did he live aloof from the popular poets of the day: Pierre-Jean de Béranger and Thomas Moore were also his favorites.

Perhaps because he was a man of feeling and action rather than a philosopher, some critics failed to read his lyrics carefully. In spite of assessments by Pál Gyulai, and later by Hugo Metzl (the professor at the University of Kolozsvar who stressed Petőfi's position in world literature in both his Hungarian and German studies), it took the work of many critics and several years to explore the full range of Petőfi's lyric. The myth of the popular figure had to be overcome, too. János Horváth's study, *Petőfi Sándor* (1922), pointed out that "Petőfi extended widely the boundaries of lyrical content, made the lyrical manner more intimate, and broke new paths in the song and the genre scenes."[3] Furthermore, he solved many of the linguistic problems that had been unresolved since the reforms of the previous generation, often by adapting the new expression to the common idiom.

Petőfi's greatest contribution to literature, however, was best expressed by István Sőtér. Following a line of argument developed by Horváth, he asserted that Petőfi created a synthesis between populism (the literary tendency to include elements derived from the ordinary people, the folk, and their culture) and romanticism which was unique not only in Hungarian literature but in world literature as well. In the process, romanticism evolved into something new. Its extreme tones and radical forms rejected the traditions of the liberal poets of the earlier age, and it became revolutionary not only in content but also in the use of daring innovations. "In its images and metaphors it follows the exaggerated, sometimes even grotesque stylistic elements of romanticism,"[4] wrote Sőtér, but it also reached into earlier traditions and revived old poetic forms. This boldness and experimentation in both form and content was to provide the impetus for the modern lyrical style of Endre Ady some fifty years later, as it was to encourage a whole new generation of poets. They did not write in Petőfi's style, and only sometimes did they touch on the same themes, but the new life and new direction that he brought to the lyric were important.

In summary, the contributions of Petőfi to Hungarian poetry were extensive: he became an ideal who inspired rather than stifled his best imitators. Moreover, the poetic world he created was natural, realistic, dignified, and still not devoid of magic, mystery, and romance. He rejected affectation and mannerism, and so could be realistic. His natural sense of decorum and propriety, on the other hand, prevented the excesses of naturalism. While never stiff, there is a certain dignity in most of his poems, due perhaps to the natural ease with which he used the spoken language and to the simple and effective poetry of his primary model, the Hungarian folksongs. The magic and romance, too, owe something to his models, but more to what has already been stated: his ability "to raise every subject to the level of poetry as naturally as if poetry was already inherent in the phenomena of the world."[5] By thus transforming common scenes and ordinary people, he taught the dignity of all men. By presenting feelings that are often allowed to drift into sentimentality with dignity and restraint, he asserted their real value. It is in these contributions, in his attitude and approach to basic human themes and problems rather than in the philosophical examination of life, that Petőfi's true value lies.

Notes and References

Preface

1. William Wordsworth, "Preface to the Second Edition of *Lyrical Ballads* (1800)," in *Selected Poems and Prefaces,* ed. Jack Stillinger (Boston: Houghton Mifflin, 1965), pp. 446–47.

Chapter One

1. Lajos Hatvany, *Igy élt Petőfi,* 2d ed. (Budapest: Akadémiai Kiadó, 1967), I, 34.
2. The summary of Petőfi's life is based mainly on the following works: Zoltán Ferenczi, *Petőfi Sándor életrajza,* 3 vols. (Budapest: Franklin Társulat, 1896); Sándor Fischer, *Petőfi élete és művei,* trans. Lajos Tolnai (Budapest: Grill, 1890); Gyula Illyés, *Petőfi Sándor* (Budapest: Szépirodalmi Könyvkiadó, 1963); Pál Pándi and Kálman Pálmai, *Petőfi Sándor* (Budapest: Gondolat, 1973) and Hatvany.
3. Pest and Buda were united to form Budapest only in 1873.
4. Sándor Petőfi to Imre Nagy, April 30, 1840, in his *Összes prózai művei és levelezése* (Budapest: Magyar Helikon, 1967), pp. 246–47. All quotations from the letters and prose of Petőfi, with the exception of the correspondence with Arany, are from this work, hereafter referred to as *Prózai művei.* They are given in my own translation. Hatvany, I, 366–67.
5. Györgyi Törő, "Petőfi anyagi helyzete," in *Tanulmányok Petőfiről,* ed. Pál Pándi and Dezső Tóth (Budapest: Akadémiai Kiadó, 1962), p. 47.
6. Petőfi to Lajos Szeberényi, November 2, 1842, in *Prózai művei,* pp. 252–53.
7. This brief survey of Hungarian literature is based on Antal Szerb, *A magyar irodalom törtenete* (Budapest: Magvető, 1959), pp. 215–32.
8. Georg Gaal, *Märchen der Magyaren* (Vienna, 1822); Johan Majlath, *Magyarische Sagen und Märchen* (Brunn, 1825); *Magyarische Gedichte* (Stuttgart, 1825); J. Majlath, G. Killian, and K. Gerold, *Blumenlese aus ungarischen Dichtern* (Pest, 1828); Julius Fenyery, Georg Tretter, and Franz Toldy, eds., *Handbuch der ungarischen*

Poesie (Pest, 1828); A. Mednyánszky, *Erzählungen, Sagen und Legenden von Ungarns Vorzeit* (Pest, 1829).

9. Cited in Illyés, p. 108.
10. Illyés, pp. 118–19.
11. István Sőtér, *Romantika és Realizmus; válogatott irodalmi tanulmányok* (Budapest: Szépirodalmi Könyvkiadó, 1965), pp. 16–17.
12. Ibid., pp. 17–18.
13. Szerb, p. 336.
14. Loránt Czigány, "*János Vitéz*: The 'People's Epic,'" in *Mosaic*, 6 (Summer, 1973), 70.
15. Cited in Pándi and Pálmai, p. 137.
16. György Spira, *Petőfi napja* (Budapest: Akadémiai Kiadó, 1975), pp. 28, 70.
17. A good account of the Revolution of 1848, with reference to Petőfi's role in it, is given in Istvan Deak, *The Lawful Revolution: Louis Kossuth and the Hungarians, 1848–1849* (New York: Columbia University Press, 1979).

Chapter Two

1. Pándi and Pálmai, pp. 28–29.
2. Sándor Petőfi, "Előszó az Összes költeményekhez," in *Prózai művei*, pp. 312–13.
3. János Arany, "A magyar nemzeti versidomról," *Prózai dolgozatok* in *Arany János Munkái*, ed. Frigyes Riedl (Budapest: Franklin Társulat, 1922), VI, 236–89.
4. Petr Rakos, *Rhythm and Metre in Hungarian Verse* (Prague: Universita Karlova, 1966).
5. János Horváth, *Rendszeres magyar verstan* (Budapest: Akadémiai Kiadó, 1951), pp. 15–51.
6. Katalin J. Soltész, "Petőfi rimei," *Magyar nyelvör*, 90 (January–March, 1966), 21.
7. Ibid., pp. 21–22.
8. Quotations are based on *Petőfi Sándor Összes költemenyei* (Budapest: Szépirodalmi Könyvkiadó, 1972). The translations are mine; the page numbers refer to this edition.
9. In Hungarian, "pearl-flower."
10. A Robin Hood type outlaw, romanticized and often supported by the people.
11. Cited in Pándi and Pálmai, p. 65.
12. Illyés, p. 139.
13. I am indebted to Loránt Czigány's essay cited above for the arguments developed here.

14. Czigány, p. 84.
15. Cited in D. Mervyn Jones, *Five Hungarian Writers* (Oxford: Clarendon Press, 1966), p. 243.

Chapter Three

1. Jenő Pintér, *Magyar irodalomtörténet* (Budapest: Magyar Irodalomtörténeti Társaság, 1930–1934), VI, 337.
2. János Horváth, *Tanulmányok* (Budapest: Akadémiai Kiadó, 1956), p. 265.
3. Sándor Petőfi, Mihály Tompa, Mór Jókai, Alajos Degre, Károly Obernyik, Albert Pálffy, Károly Berczy, Albert Pákh, Kálmán Lisznyai, Frigyes Kerényi.
4. "A csárda romjai."
5. The *délibáb* is a mirage that appears on the great plains, showing cities and fantastic scenes, all upside-down.
6. Horváth, *Tanulmányok*, p. 229.
7. Ibid., p. 315.
8. Ibid., p. 316.
9. Petőfi to Arany, February 4, 1847, in *Arany és Petőfi levelezése*, ed. László Szíjgyárto (Budapest: Mora, 1959), p. 11.

Chapter Four

1. Horváth, *Tanulmányok*, p. 300.
2. Illyés considers this one of the greatest lyrical poems in world literature and fully deserving of the more than fifty translations it has inspired,p. 278.
3. Illyés, p. 279.
4. The parallelism of the autumnal mountains and the poet's graying hair are more striking in Hungarian since "ősz" means both "autumn" and "gray."
5. Illyés, p. 320.
6. Horváth, *Tanulmányok*, p. 311.
7. In the thirteenth century, the Tatar invasion laid waste the country and gave rise to this idiomatic expression for utter devastation and neglect.
8. Frederick Riedl, *A History of Hungarian Literature* (London: Heineman, 1906), p. 204.

Chapter Five

1. Petőfi to Arany, February 4, 1847, *Arany és Petőfi levelezése*, p. 11.

2. Arany to Petőfi, pp. 14–17.

3. Mátyás (Matthias) Hunyadi (1458–1490), son of János Hunyadi, a nobleman, was elected king by acclamation; he was considered a just king and a champion of the people against the powerful magnates.

4. Máté Csák, a famous leader in the Highlands, regarded as a brigand or as a revolutionary. Ferenc Rákóczi (1705–1711), prince of Transylvania and leader of a revolt against Austria.

5. *Prózai művei*, pp. 312–13.

6. Note by Arany in *Arany és Petőfi levelezése*, pp. 42–43.

7. "Arany Lacinak."

8. Note by Arany, in *Arany és Petőfi levelezése*, p. 42.

9. Zsolt Beöthy, *A magyar irodalom története*, 2d ed. (Budapest: Athenaeum, 1899–1900), II, 285.

10. A tributary of the Tisza River.

11. Riedl, p. 208.

12. Ibid.

Chapter Six

1. Arany to Petőfi, June 27, 1848, pp. 114–49.

2. "A népbarát programja," p. 414; "A Kis-Kúnokhoz," pp. 418–21; "Nyilatkozat a szabadszállási választás ügyében," June 15, 1848, pp. 423–31; "A szabadszállási néphez," End of June, 1848, pp. 432–33; articles in *Életképek*, June 11, 1848, pp. 415–18 and *Március Tizenötödike*, June 19, 1848. Page references are to *Prózai művei*.

3. Arany to Petőfi, April 22, 1848, pp. 136–37.

4. Petőfi to Arany, July 1, 1848, p. 152.

5. Petőfi to Arany, August 16, p. 165.

6. Ibid.

7. See chapter 8 for a discussion of Petőfi's influence on these two German poets, and Enikő I. Molnár, "Hungarian Influences in German Literature up to Petőfi" (M.A. thesis, University of North Carolina, Chapel Hill, 1965), pp. 212–34.

8. János Hunyadi, Regent of Hungary, 1446–1452; father of King Matthias (see chapter 5, note 3), and the hero of Nándorfehérvár (Belgrade) against the Turks in 1456.

9. Miklós Zrinyi, the captain of the fortress of Szigetvár, who died in its defense in 1564, but succeeded in stopping the Turkish advance considerably short of Vienna; his grandnephew, also Miklós (1620–1664), author of an epic commemorating the deeds of his ancestor, was also a military commander against the Turks. Uncle of Ferenc Rákóczi II.

10. See chapter 5, note 4.
11. "Első esküm."
12. Horváth, *Tanulmányok*, p. 311.
13. Illyés, pp. 349–50.
14. Articles in *Életkepek*, June 11, 1848, pp. 415–18; in *Március Tizenötödike*, September 18, 1848, pp. 458–62; page references are to *Prózai művei*.
15. Pándi and Pálmai, p. 323.
16. "Az Egyenlőségi Társulat Proklamációja," pp. 458–62; "Lapok Petőfi Sándor naplójából, pp. 407–8; articles in *Életképek*, June 11, 1848, pp. 417–18; page references are to *Prózai művei*.
17. Illyés, p. 405.

Chapter Seven

1. "Ti akácfák a kertben."
2. Cited in Illyés, p. 479.
3. "Szülőföldemen"; "Kiskúnság."
4. "Fiam születésére"; Szüleim halálára."
5. "A hegyek közt"; "Itt van az ősz, itt van ujra"; "Elpusztuló kert ott a vár alatt."
6. His father died of typhoid on March 21, 1849; his mother of cholera on May 17, 1849, during the siege of Buda. Both were in a sense victims of the war. Petőfi was in Debrecen and eastern Hungary in these months.
7. "Rákóczi."
8. "A nemzetgyűléshez."
9. "Akasszátok fel a királyokat"; "Itt a nyilam, mibe lőjjem?"
10. Literally, "Field of Blood," but also a region of Buda, below the royal castle, the site of executions.
11. An ethnic Hungarian group, one of the "nations" of Transylvania with their own military and civil organization; they enjoyed the privileges of the nobility as a group, though were severely restricted under Austrian rule.
12. "A Szabadsághoz."
13. Imre Vahot, *Nemzetőr*, September 10, 1848, cited in Pintér, p. 328.
14. Letter to the editor of the *Közlöny*, April 17, 1849, in *Prózai művei*, pp. 495–96.
15. Letter to the editor of the *Közlöny*, February 15, 1849, *Prózai művei*, pp. 487–89.
16. Letter to the Parliament, December 8, 1848, *Prózai művei*, pp. 473. The "Csatadal" was enclosed in this letter.

17. Hatvany cites Miklós Gyarmati, a soldier who recounted his remembrances in *Kolozsvár,* December 24, 1890, and Károly P. Szathmáry, *Vasárnapi Ujság,* no. 50 (1890), 811. Both these sources refer to the battle of Vízakna.

18. Here and in the next few poems I have kept the term "Magyar" for "Hungarian" as it seemed to me to evoke Petőfi's meaning more closely. It should be remembered, however, that the terms are interchangeable, and "Magyar" is not meant to refer to only one of the ethnic groups comprising the Hungarian nation—such an interpretation would do violence to Petőfi's text.

Chapter Eight

1. József Túróczi-Trostler, "*Petőfi belép a világirodalomba,* trans. Arpád Berczik and Ilona Komor (Budapest: Akadémiai Kiadó, 1974), pp. 197–201.
2. Cited in Victor Clement, trans. *The Apostle, a Narrative Poem* (1848), by Sándor Petőfi (Budapest: Corvina, 1961), foreword.
3. József Kiss, "Petőfi az egykorú német-nyelvű sajtóban 1844–1846," in Pándi and Toth, pp. 120–21.
4. Ibid., p. 93.
5. *Pester Zeitung,* no. 129 (1845).
6. Heinrich Heine, *Briefwechsel,* ed. Friedrich Hirth (Berlin: Propyläenverlag, 1920), III, 90.
7. Heinrich Heine, *Samtliche Werke* (Hamburg: Hoffman & Campe, 1876), VII, 103–4.
8. "Long live the Fatherland!"
9. Bettina von Arnim, *Werke und Briefe,* ed. Gusztav Konrad (Frechen: Bartmann, 1963), III, 302.
10. Ibid., p. 368.
11. Karl Maria Kertbény, *Silhouetten und Reliquien* (Vienna and Prague: Kober and Markgraf, 1861), pp. 105–21.
12. Túróczi-Trostler, *Petőfi belép,* pp. 201–7.
13. Georg Geohler, "Friedrich Nietzsches Kompositionen zu Gedichten von Petőfi," *Ungarische Jahrbucher,* 3 (1923), 175.
14. Rezső Boros, "Petőfi-Lieder in der romantischen Musik Deutschlands," *Acta Litteraria,* 2 (1959), 416.
15. Molnár, appendix C.
16. *Gedichte,* trans. Martin Remane, 2d ed. (Budapest: Corvina, 1973).
17. Kertbény, pp. 105–21.
18. John Bowring, trans., *Translations from Alexander Petőfi, the Magyar Poet* (London: Trubner, 1866), preface, pp. 10–11.

19. Francis and Theresa Pulszky, *Tales and Traditions of Hungary* (London, 1851); Henry Curwen, *Sorrow and Song, Studies* (London, 1875); Henry Phillips, *Selections from the Poems of Alexander Petőfi* (Philadelphia, 1885); E. D. Butler, *The Legend of the Wondrous Hunt* (London, 1881).

20. William N. Loew, *Gems from Petőfi and Other Hungarian Poets* (New York, 1881); *Magyar Songs* (New York, 1887); *Magyar Poetry* (New York, 1899); *Alexander Petőfi* (New York, 1912); *Childe John* (Budapest, 1920); *Modern Magyar Lyrics* (Budapest, 1926).

21. Eugenie Bayard Pierce and Emil Delmar, trans. (Budapest: Petőfi Society, 1948).

22. Watson Kirkconnell, trans., *The Magyar Muse* (Winnipeg: Kanadai Magyar Ujság, 1933); Jozsef Grosz and W. Arthur Boggs, trans., *Hungarian Anthology: A Collection of Poems*, 2d ed. rev. (Toronto: Pannonia, 1966).

23. *Magyar Irodalmi Lexicon*, ed, Benedek Marcell (Budapest: Akadémiai Kiadó, 1963–1965).

Conclusion

1. Pál Gyulai, "Petőfi Sándor és lyrai költészetünk," in *Irodalmi Tanulmányok*, vol. 3 of *Munkái* (Budapest: Kisfaludi Társaság, n.d.), pp. 6–52.

2. Ibid., p. 44.

3. Cited in Pintér, p. 400.

4. Sőtér, p. 216.

5. Czigány, p. 70.

Selected Bibliography

PRIMARY SOURCES

1. First Editions

Only monographs are included here, as individual poems and occasional publications are too numerous to be listed. Full listing of these works can be found in: Zoltán Ferenczi, comp., "Petőfi-kiadások, 1843–1897," in *Petőfi-album* (Budapest, Athenaeum, 1898); József Szinnyei, *Petőfi Sándor* (Budapest: V. Hornyanszky, 1950); and *Petőfi napja a magyar irodalomban: 1842–1848*, comp., Sándor Endrődi (Budapest: Petőfi Társaság, 1911).

a. Original Works

A helység kalapácsa: Hősköltemény négy énekben. Pest: Geibel, 1844.
Versek. 1842–1844. Buda: Magyar Királyi Egyetem Betűivel, 1844.
Cipruslombok Etelke sírjáról. Pest: Beimel, 1845.
János vitéz. Buda: Magyar Királyi Egyetem Betűivel, 1845.
Szerelem gyöngyei. Pest: Landerer és Heckenast, 1845.
Versek: 1844–1845. Pest: Beimel, 1845.
Felhők. Pest, 1846.
A hóhér kötele. Pest: Hartleben, 1846.
Összes költeményei. Pest: G. Emich, 1847.
Tigris és hiéna. Pest: G. Emich, 1847.
Ujabb költenméyei: 1847–1849. Pest: G. Emich, 1851.

b. Translations

A koros hölgy. By Charles Bernard. Pest, 1843. From French.
Robin Hood. By George James. Pest, 1844. From English.
Coriolanus. Pest, 1848. From English. Based on play by Shakespeare.

2. Collected Works

Vegyes művei. 1838–1849. Edited by Pál Gyulai. 3 vols. Pest: Pfeiffer, 1863.
Ujabb költeményei. 1847–1849. 4th ed. 2 vols. Budapest: Athenaeum, 1873.

Költeményei. Edited by Agost Gregus and Pál Gyulai. Budapest: Athenaeum, 1874.
Összes művek. Edited by Adolf Havas. 6 vols. Budapest: Athenaeum, 1892–1896. Critical edition.
Munkái. Edited by Ferenc Badics. 4 vols. Budapest: Franklin Társulat, 1906.
Levelei. Edited by Ferenc Badics. Budapest: Petőfi Konyvtár, 1910.
Összes költeményei. Edited by Géza Voinovich. 2 vols. Budapest: Franklin Társulat, 1921.
Összes költeményei. Introduction by Gyula Pekar. Budapest: Petőfi-Társaság, 1933. Omits many poems with revolutionary themes.
Összes művei. Budapest: Frankin Társulat, 1941.
Összes költeményei: 1838–1844. Edited by Béla Varjas. Budapest: Budapest Székfőváros, 1948. Only printed volume of a planned complete edition of his works.
Válogatott prózai irásai. Budapest: Franklin Könyvkiadó, 1950.
Összes Művei. 7 vols. Budapest: Akadémiai Kiadó, 1951–. Critical edition.
Összes művei. Edited by Pál Pándi. 3 vols. Magyar Klasszikusok. Budapest: Szépirodalmi Könyvkiadó, 1955.
Összes költeményei. 2 vols. Budapest: Szépirodalmi Könyvkiadó, 1959.
Összes prózai művei és levelezése. Edited by Pál Pándi. Budapest: Szépirodalmi Könyvkiadó, 1960.
Összes költeményei. Budapest: Magyar Helikon, 1967.
Összes költeményei. Budapest: Szépirodalmi Könyvkiadó, 1972.
Útirajzok. Úti jegyzetek (1845): Úti levelek. Budapest: Magyar Helikon, 1962.
Vers és próza. Budapest: Magvető, 1972. Selections.

3. English Translations

Alexander Petőfi: The Apostle, Childe John, Simple Steve, Cypress Leaves from the Grave of Dear Ethel, Selected Lyrics. Translated by William N. Loew. New York: Hungarian Literary Society, 1912.
The Apostle, A Narrative Poem, 1848. Translated by Victor Clement. Budapest: Corvina, 1961.
Childe John. Translated by William N. Loew. Budapest: Hungarian Studio, 1920.
Evadne and Other Poems. Translated by Frederick W. Fuller. London: K. Paul, 1894.
Petőfi Sándor by Himself. Introduction by György Radó. Translated

by George F. Cushing, E. B. Pierce et al. Budapest: Pannonia, 1973.

Rebel or Revolutionary? Sándor Petőfi as Revealed by His Diary, Letters, Notes, Pamphlets and Poems. Foreword by Bela Köpeczi. Translated by Edwin Morgan and G. F. Cushing. Budapest: Corvina, 1974.

Selections from the Poems of Alexander Petőfi. Translated by Henry Phillips. Philadelphia: Privately printed, 1885.

Sixty Poems. Translated by E. B. Pierce and E. Delmar. Budapest: Petőfi Society, 1949.

Translations from Alexander Petőfi, the Magyar Poet. Translated by John Bowring. London: Trubner, 1866.

4. Anthologies Containing English Translations

GROSZ, JOSEPH, and BOGGS, W. ARTHUR, trans. *Hungarian Anthology: a Collection of Poems.* 2d ed. rev. Toronto: Pannonia, 1966.

KIRKCONNELL, WATSON, trans. *The Magyar Muse: An Anthology of Hungarian Poetry, 1400–1932.* Winnipeg: Kanadai Magyar Ujsag, 1933.

LOEW, WILLIAM N., trans. *Gems from Petőfi and Other Hungarian Poets.* New York: Paul O. D'Esterhazy, 1881.

——. *Magyar Poetry: Selections from Hungarian Poets.* New York: Amerikai Magyar Népszava, 1908.

——. *Modern Magyar Lyrics; Selected Gems from Petőfi and Other Hungarian Poets.* Budapest: Wodianer, 1926.

SECONDARY SOURCES

1. Studies in English

CZIGÁNY, LORÁNT. "*János Vitéz,* The 'People's Epic.'" *Mosaic,* 6 (Summer, 1973), 69–87. A careful analysis of the poem in terms of populist literature.

ILLYÉS, GYULA. *Petőfi.* Translated by G. F. Cushing. Budapest: Covina, 1973. Biography of the poet with extensive citations of his works used to evaluate his life, and the use of biographical facts in the evaluation of his works; sensitive analysis of the poetry.

JONES, DAVID MERVYN. *Five Hungarian Writers.* Oxford: Clarendon Press, 1966. Contains one of the best critical studies of the poet.

KLANICZAY, TIBOR, SZAUDER, JÓZSEF, and SZABOLCSI, MIKLÓS. *History of Hungarian Literature.* Budapest: Corvina, 1964. The only recent history of Hungarian literature available in English, but unfortunately limited in scope and offering little beyond generalities.

RADÓ, GYÖRGY. "Petőfi Abroad." *New Hungarian Quarterly*, 49 (Spring, 1973), 60–71. Review of the early or important translations of Petőfi in Europe and America.

REMÉNYI, JOSEPH. *Hungarian Writers and Literature: Modern Novelists, Critics and Poets.* New Brunswick, N.J.: Rutgers University Press, 1964. A perceptive essay on the man and the poet; his meaning for Hungarian literature is given in the chapter on Petőfi.

RIEDL, FREDERICK. *A History of Hungarian Literature.* 1906. Reprint ed., Detroit: Gale Research Co., 1968. A still useful study of Hungarian literature through the nineteenth century.

SŐTÉR, ISTVÁN. Sándor Petőfi, Folk Poet and Revolutionary." *New Hungarian Quarterly*, 49 (Spring, 1973), 54–59. Petőfi as a poetic innovator who used his talents in the service of the Revolution. Stresses the unity of Petőfi's art, but occasionally wrenches facts to make them conform to the revolutionary thesis.

YOLLAND, ARTHUR B. *Alexander Petőfi, Poet of the Hungarian War of Independence: A Literary Study 1823–1849.* Considers the nature and characteristics of his poetry as well as his life.

2. Studies in Hungarian

ADY, ENDRE. *"Petőfi nem alkuszik."* In *Válogatott cikkei és tanulmányai.* Edited by Gyula Földessy. Budapest: Szépirodalmi Könyvkiadó, 1954. Emphasizes the radical aspects of the life and poetry of Petőfi, with attention to his ideas, feelings, and marriage.

Alföld, no. 1 (1973). The issue is devoted to Petőfi and contains a variety of writings on him.

BORI, IMRE. *Szövegértelmezések: irások versekről, prózáról.* Ujvidék: Forum, 1977. Several chapters are devoted to the analysis of Petőfi's writings; good textual criticism.

ERDÉLYI, JÁNOS. "Petőfi Sándor." In *Pályák és Pálmak.* Budapest: Franklin Társulat, 1886. One of the earliest critical assessments of the poet, concentrates on his character, creativity and connection with the literature of his age.

FERENCZI, ZOLTÁN. *Petőfi Sándor életrajza,* 3 vols. Budapest: Franklin Társulat, 1896. Good biography, with some critical insight into the forces that shaped the poet.

FISCHER, SÁNDOR. *Petőfi élete és művei.* Introduction by Mór Jókai. Translated from the German by Lajos Tolnai. Budapest: Grill,

1890. The standard biography for years, it contains some legendary material, but also gives attention to his works.

Filológiai Közlöny, nos. 1–2 (1973). The issue is devoted to Petőfi.

Forrás (1973). *Petőfi különszám.* Also a special issue devoted to Petőfi, contains articles on the poet and his works.

FRIED, ISTVÁN, and SZAPPANOS, BALÁZS. *Petőfi-versek elemzése.* Budapest: Tankönyvkiadó, 1978. *Explication de texte* and critical study for secondary school students designed to raise their appreciation of literature and Petőfi.

GYULAI, PÁL. *Petőfi Sándor és lyrai költészetünk.* Budapest: Kunossy, Szilágyi és Társa, 1908. First published in 1854 (*Uj Magyar Muzeum*); first essay to point out the lyrical innovations of Petőfi and to attempt to evaluate his literary merit. A more sympathetic picture of the poet than is given in Erdélyi.

HATVANY, LAJOS. *Így élt Petőfi.* 2d ed. 2 vols. Budapest: Akadémiai Kiadó, 1967. A compilation of biographical sources with citations from contemporaries and documentary evidence based on previously published scholarship.

HORVÁTH, JÁNOS. *Petőfi Sándor.* Budapest: Pallas, 1922. The character of the lyric poems through the changes in the development of the poet's style.

——. *Tanulmányok.* Budapest: Akadémiai Kiadó, 1956. The studies contain an analysis of Petőfi's poetry in terms of the above, his innovations in style, and his poetic stance.

Irodalomtörténet, no. 1 (1973). Articles on Petőfi in this anniversary issue.

Irodalomtörténeti Közlemények, nos. 1–2 (1973). Anniversary issue for Petőfi.

Jelenkor, no. 1 (1973). Anniversary issue for Petőfi.

KIRÁLY, ISTVÁN. "Petőfi mint vízválasztó." *Irodalomtörténet,* 38, no. 2 (1949), 169–83. The three stages of the development of a critical picture of Petőfi between 1849 and the early twentieth century.

Kortárs, no. 1 (1973). Petőfi issue.

LUKÁCSY, SÁNDOR, and VARGA, JÁNOS, eds. *Petőfi és kora.* Budapest: Akadémiai Kiadó, 1970. Essays on various aspects of Petőfi's age, with emphasis on the political situation. The evaluation tends to be in terms of Marxist positivism.

MARTINKÓ, ANDRÁS. *Költő, mű és környezet; kérdőjelek a Petőfi irodalomban.* Budapest: Akadémiai Kiadó, 1973. Critical reevaluation of some problems in the Petőfi literature.

Nyugat, 16 (January 1, 1923). Memorial issue, contains several critical essays on his poetry and works.

PANDI, PÁL. *Első aranykorunk: cikkek, tanulmányok a magyar fel-*

világosodás és reformkor irodalmáról. Budapest: Szépirodalmi Könyvkiadó, 1976. About half the volume is devoted to Petőfi, with the essays emphasizing political and national considerations in the work of the poet.

——, and PÁLMAI, KÁLMÁN. *Petőfi Sándor.* Nagy magyar irok. Budapest: Gondolat, 1973. A study of the poet's work in terms of socialist literary criticism.

——, and TOTH, DEZSŐ. eds. *Tanulmányok Petőfiről.* Irodalomtörténeti Könyvtár, no. 9. Budapest: Akadémiai Kiadó, 1962. A collection of informative and well-researched articles on various aspects of his poetry and prose.

Petőfi-Album. Edited by Lajos Bartok, Sandor Endrődi, and Tamás Szana. Budapest: Athenaeum, 1898. Studies of his life and works.

Petőfi Irodalmi Múzeum. Évkönyve 10. 1823–1973. A memorial issue.

Petőfi Könyvtár. Edited by Sándor Endrődi and Zoltán Ferenczi. 30 pamphlets. Budapest: Kunossy, Szilágyi és Társa, 1908–1911. Contains biographical and literary studies of the poet.

Petőfi-Mozaik. Edited by Rózsa Paál and Antal Weber. Budapest: Tankönyvkiadó, 1975. Papers presented for the one hundred and fiftieth anniversary of the poet at the Eötvös Lorand University and at meetings in Kecskemét.

Petőfi Tüze: tanulmányok Petőfi Sándorról. Edited by Anna Tamás and Antal Weber. Budapest: Kossuth Könyvkiadó, 1972. A collection of critical essays.

Petőfitől, Petőfiről: a költő születésének 150. évfordulóján. Compiled by Mrs. Béla Czuth and Mrs. Zoltán Esik. Selection of writings by Petőfi about himself and by others, including contemporaries, about him.

PINTÉR, JÉNŐ. *Magyar irodalomtörténet.* 7 vols. Budapest: Magyar Irodalomtörténeti Társaság, 1930–1934. Detailed study of the poet: criticism, background, publications, and a detailed bibliography.

RIEDL, FREDERICK. *Petőfi Sándor.* Budapest: Franklin Társulat, 1923. His life and works, the effect of his times on his development and the relationship between his writings and European romanticism.

SOTÉR, ISTVÁN. *Romantika és realizmus; válogatott irodalmi tanulmányok.* Budapest: Szépirodalmi Könyvkiadó, 1956. A study of the basic realism of Petőfi's work within the framework of Hungarian romanticism and realism.

——. "Uj Petőfi-kép." In *Az ember és műve: tanulmányok.* Budapest: Akadémiai Kiadó, 1971. A survey of the critical literature on Petőfi.

SZERB, ANTAL. *Magyar irodalomtörténet.* Budapest: Magvető, 1957.

Detailed study of the influences and figures that shaped Hungarian literature, with the section on Petőfi (pp. 368–90) devoted to the survey of the various themes and styles found in the works of the poet.

TÚRÓCZI-TROSTLER, JÓZSEF. *Petőfi belép a világirodalomba.* Translated by Árpád Berczik and Ilona Komor. Budapest: Akadémiai Kiadó, 1974. A detailed study of the interest in Petőfi outside of Hungary, particularly in Germany and the German-speaking lands.

Index

Alföld, 15, 24, 98, 99, *102–103*, 104, 105, 109
Arany, János, 27, 30, 31, 35, 77, 86, *94–97*, 111, 112
Arnim, Bettina von, 113, 160, 163, *165–66*, 167
Athenaeum, 21 22
Aurora, 19, 20, 21, 27

Bajza, József, 16, 20, 21, 34
Bánk Bán (Katona), 21
Bem, General József, 33, 139, 148, *152–54*
Béranger, Pierre-Jean de, 26, 28, 65, 164, 169
Berzsenyi, Dániel, 16, 18, 19
Bessenyei, György, 18
Bowring, Sir John, 166–67
Byron, George Gordon, Lord, 28, 65, 102

Clouds. See Felhők
Collected Poems. See Összes költeményei
Committee of Safety, 126, 147
Coriolanus (Shakespeare), 28, 33
Csapó, Etelke, 28, 62
csárda, 69, 70, 98, 99, 100, 103
Csokonai Vitéz, Mihály, 16, 17, 19, 65
Cypress Leaves from the Tomb of Etelke. See Cipruslombok Etelke sírjáról

Dux, Adolf, 160, *161–62*, 166

Életképek, 27, 29, 30, 33, 83, 94, 147
Enlightenment, 17, 18, 20, 28
Erdély. *See* Transylvania
Erdélyi, János, 27
"Europe Is Quiet, Quiet Again." *See* "Európa csendes, ujra csendes."

Goethe, Johann Wolfgang von, 25, 28
Great Hungarian Plain. *See Alföld*
Great Plain. *See Alföld*
Gvadányi, József, 16, 18, 42
Gyulai, Pál, 27

Habsburg, 16, 21, 25, 27, 32, 70, 86, 92, 115, 116, 117, 118, 120, 122, 126, 143, 144
Hammer of the Village, The. See A helység kalapácsa
Hazánk, 31, 32
Heine, Heinrich, 34, 65, 113, 161, *163–65*, 169
Horace, 34
Hruz, Mária, 15, 43. *See also* Petrovics, István
Hugo, Victor, 25, 28

Jókai, Mór, 17, 26, 27, 94, 121, 122

Katona, József, 21
Kazinczy, Ferenc, 18, 19, 26
Keats, John, 61, 74, 102
Kemény, Zsigmond, 27
Kertbény, Karl Maria, 160, 161, *162–64*, 166
Kisfaludi, Károly, 19, 20, 34, 47
Kisfaludi, Társaság, 21, 22, 94
Kölcsey, Ferenc, 20, 25, 26, 69, 115
Kossuth, Lajos, 25, 32, 120, 123

Lamartine, Alphonse de, 28
Lenau, Nicholas, 33, 98
Lowlands. *See Alföld*

March Youth, 121. *See also* "Márciusi ifjak"
Martinovics revolt, 18, 145
Mednyánszky, Berta, 29, 63
Moore, Thomas, 28, 169

National Ode. *See* "Nemzeti dal"
National Theater, 21–22, 29
Nemzeti Kör, 23
Novalis, 62, 72

Pearls of Love, The. See Szerelem gyöngyei
Pesti Divatlap, 23, 24, 27, 28, 39, 47
Petőfi, Sándor
WORKS: POETRY
"A borozó," 37
"A csárda romjai," 69–71
"A csonka torony," 95
"A faluban utcahosszat," 38
"A farkasok dala," 118
"A hazáról," 68–69
"A hegyek között," 141
A helység kalapácsa, 28, *46–50*
"A honvéd," 152
"A két ország ölelkezése," 143
"A király esküje," 144
"A királyokhoz," 126, 143
"A kisbéres," 93
"A kutyák dala," 118
"A ledőlt szobor," 143
"A magyar nemes," 67–68, 92
"A magyarok istene," 157–58
"A márciusi ifjak," 143
"A munkácsi várban," 118
"A négy-ökrös szekér," 71–72
"A nép nevében," 119
"A puszta télen," 105–106
"A szabadsághoz," 146
"A székelyekhez," 146
"A tavaszhoz," 141–42
"A téli esték," 93, 98, 101
"A Tisza," 106–108
"A XIX. század költői," 113
"A vándor," 92
"A vén zaszlótartó," 151
"A virágnak megtiltani nem lehet," 40–41
"Árvalányhaj a süvegem bokrétája," 38–39
"Augusztus 5.-én," 84–85
"Ausztria," 144
"Az Alföld," 120
"Az apostol," 111, *127–34*
"Az erdélyi hadsereg," 153
"Az országgyűléshez," 124
"Az őrült," 66–67
"Az én Pegazusom," 114
"Bánk bán," 144
"Befordúltam a konyhára," 38, 39
"Bírom végre Juliskámat," 635
"Bizony mondom, hogy győz most a magyar," 149
"Bolond Istók," *90–92*, 101
"Bordal," 150–55
"Búcsú," 139
Cipruslombok Etelke sírjáról, 28, *62–63*
"Csalogányok és pacsírták," 116
"Csatadal," 154
"Dalaim," 76
"Dobzse László," 144
"Egri hangok," 23, 38, 77, 115
"Egy estém otthon," 43
"Egy gondolat bánt engemet," 112–13
"Egy telem Debrecenben," 45
"Élet vagy halál," 146
"Elpusztuló kert ott a vár alatt," 141
"Erdélyben," 117–18
"1848 [Ezernyolcszanegyvennyolc]," 146–47
"Europa csendes, ujra csendes," 148–49, 164
"Falu végén kurta kocsma," 98, 100–101
"Fekete-piros dal," 146
"*Felhők*," 29, 66, 73
"Feleségem és kardom," 136–37
"Fiam születésére," 140
"Föl!" 155
"Föl a szent háborúra!," 155–56

"Fürdik a holdvilág az ég tengerében," 41–42
"Füstbement terv," 43
"Ha férfi vagy, légy férfi," 114
"Hallod-e szív, szivem!," 147
"Hány hét a világ?," 146
"Három madár," 137
"Hazámban," 34
"Hideg idő, hűs őszi éj," 135
"Hogy volna kedvem," 135
"Hol a leány, ki lelkem röpülését," 84
"Honfidal," 115
"Hortobágyi kocsmárosné," 37
"Hozzám jösz-e?," 84
"Ismét magyar lett a magyar," 146
"István öcsémhez," 43–44
"Itt benn vagyok a férfikor nyarában," 137–39
"Itt van az ősz, itt van ujra," 141
János Vitéz, 28, 46, 50–60, 100
"Kellemetlen őszi reggel," 80
"Két orszag ölelkezése," 127
"Ki gondolná, ki mondaná," 142–43
"Kiskunság," 104–105
"Kit feledni vágytam," 83–84
"Kont és társai," 144
"Kun László krónikája," 144
"Kutyakaparó," 98–100
"Lenkei százada," 150–51
"Levél Várady Antalhoz," 75–76
"Lopott ló," 42
"Magyar vagyok," 117
"Már minékünk ellenségünk," 146
Miért kisérsz," 141
"Miért zárjatok el utamat?," 144
"Milyen lárma, milyen vigadalom," 155
"Minek nevezzelek," 89
"Mit daloltok még," 147
"Mit nem beszél a német," 146
"Megint beszélünk, megint csak beszélünk," 124
"Muzsám és mennyaszonyom," 85
"Nemzeti dal," 32, 121, *124–25*
Összes költeményei, 29, 30, 46, 96
Összes versei. *See* Összzes költeményei
"Pacsirtaszót hallok megint," 142
"Pató Pál úr," 92
"Reszket a bokor, mert," *81–83*, 169
"Rosz verseimről," 45
"Rózsabokor a domboldalon," 88–89
Salgó, 65
"Sári néni," 96–97, 101
"Sors, nyiss nekem tért," 76
"Széchy Mária," 95–96
"Szeget szeggel," 42
"Szeptember végen," *86–88*, 109
"Szerelem gyöngyei," 29, *63–64*
"Szerelmes vagyok," 79, 80
"Szeretlek, kedvesem," 89
"Szilaj Pista," 65
"Szüleim halálára," 140–41
"Szülőföldemen," 109–10
Táblabíró, 92
"Te az enyém, én a tiéd," 84
"Te vagy, te vagy," 80
"Ti akácfák a kertben," 136
"Tigris és hiéna," 29, 30, 65
"Tiszteljétek a közkatonákat," 151
"Tudod, midőn elöször ültünk," 136
"Tündérálom," *72–74*, 78
"Uton vagyok, s nem vagy velem," 135
"Vajdahunyadon," 153–54
"Válasz, kedvesem levelére," 85
"Van-e mostan olyan legeny," 126, 155
"Vándorélet," 42
"Vasúton," 115
"Vérmező," 144–45
Versek 1842–1844, 22, 28

WORKS: PROSE
"A fakó legény és a pej leány," 101–102
A hóhér kötele, 29, 65, 102
"A nagyapa," 101
"Uti jegyzetek," 29, *64–67*, 111

"Uti levelek Kerényi Frigyeshez," 31, 111
Zöld Marci, 29, 65

Petrovics, István, 15, 23–24, 43–44, 66, 113, 140, 151
plains. *See puszta*
Poems 1842–1844. *See* Versek 1842–1844
prairie. *See puszta*
Pulszky, Ferenc, 27
puszta, 38, 53, 69, 70, 90, 103, 104, 105, 106, 114, 160

Reform Era, 24, 25, 26, 50, 111
Reform Movement. *See* Reform Era
Revolution of 1848, 26, 27, 32–33, 69, 86, 111–12, 113, 118, 119, *120–27*, *135–59*, 162, 165
Romanticism, 17, 25, 26, 47, 61, 72–73, 74, 78, 102, 115

Schiller, Friedrich, 25, 34, 65
Shakespeare, William, 28, 33, 65, 169
Shelley, Percy Bysshe, 28, 61, 65, 76, 146, 169
Society of Ten. *See* Tizek Társasága
Strick des Henkers, Der. *See A hóhér kötele*
Szeberényi, Lajos, 17
Széchenyi, Ferenc, 19
Széchenyi, Istvan, 19, 25, 32, 120, 121
Székely, 146, 148, 151–52
Szendrey, Júlia (wife), 29, 30, 79–89, 135, 136–40, 141

Teleki, Count, 30, 31, 85
Tiger and Hyena. *See Tigris és hiena*
Tinodi Lantos, Sebestyén, 37
Tizek, Társasága, 29, 66
Tizenkét Pont, 32, 120, 121, *122*
Tompa, Mihály, 27
Transylvania, 19, 31, 33, 85–86, 117, 122, 127, 139, 140, 148, 150, 151, 153
"Travel Notes." *See* "Uti jegyzetek"
"Travel Notes to Frigyes Kerenyi." *See* "Uti levelek Kerényi Frigyeshez"
Twelve Points. *See* Tizenkét Pont

Vachot brothers, 27, 47, 66, 147
Vaterland. *See Hazánk*
Vörösmarty, Mihály, 16, 18, 20, 21, 22, 25, 26, 34, 47, 69, 78, 115

War of Independence. *See* Revolution of 1848
Wordsworth, William, 102

Young, Edward, 62

Zrinyi, Miklos, 37